THE LOVE FOR THREE ORANGES
Based on the opera by Sergei Prokofiev (1891-1953)

"I'm in love with oranges three
And I'll find them, just wait and see."

So sang young Prince Tartaly as he set out for the Kingdom of the Giant Cook who kept three magic oranges in her Terrible Kitchen. This delightful fairy-tale opera by the composer of *Peter and the Wolf* was first performed over forty years ago, in Chicago. Since that time, audiences of all ages and all over the world have been laughing at Prince Tartaly's misadventures, and enjoying Prokofiev's bubbling score.

The present adaptation marks the first time that this modern classic is presented especially for young readers. Mme. Lina Prokofiev, the composer's wife, has provided an introduction, and the story text has been carefully read by the Metropolitan Opera Guild for accuracy and fidelity to the original.

We present then, for your pleasure, THE LOVE FOR THREE ORANGES.

Other books in this series:

AIDA

THE BARBER OF SEVILLE

LOHENGRIN

In cooperation with
The Metropolitan Opera Guild, Inc.

Based on the opera by
Sergei Prokofiev

The Love for Three Oranges

Retold by John Moreton
Illustrated by Murray Tinkelman
With an introduction by Mme. Prokofiev

Dedicated to
Peter and Tom Lenz

A NOTE FROM MME. PROKOFIEV

I first saw Sergei Prokofiev in New York, performing his piano concerti at Carnegie Hall. It was shortly after the First World War and Prokofiev had left Russia only a short time before. His performance and the originality of his music made a deep impression upon me. His inner concentration was remarkable. He was very tall and thin, and when he bowed to his audience, one thought he would break in half. We had some friends in common, among them the composer Rachmaninoff, and we met frequently. Even than I was struck by Prokofiev's capacity for work. I felt that he was a born fighter. But he was also an optimist, a man of great inner strength, always gay and quick-witted, a lively and fascinating conversationalist.

His first opera to be produced, THE LOVE FOR THREE ORANGES, was soon to be premiered at the Chicago Lyric Opera. It was based on a comedy by the eighteenth-century Italian playwright Carlo Gozzi. The play had first attracted Prokofiev's attention in a Russian theater magazine, and it accompanied him when he left Russia to travel abroad. In developing THE LOVE FOR THREE ORANGES into an opera, Prokofiev used the format of the Italian *Commedia dell' Arte*, utilizing the clowns of the old Italian comedy theater. Prokofiev had been composing since childhood, including an early opera written at the age of nine. The work was presented at his grandfather's house by an enthusiastic cast of relatives. At the conclusion, the boy's grandfather joked, "Sergei, when they perform your works in the Imperial Theater someday, remember that your first opera was

presented in my house." Prokofiev remembered those words twenty years later, when THE LOVE FOR THREE ORANGES was about to be presented in Chicago.

The libretto for the delightful ORANGES was written by Prokofiev himself. He developed personally the dramatization of the opera and changed some of the original play's staging. Many of the comic touches were his own. In spite of interruption by illness and a postponement of the opening, work on the ORANGES went ahead.

At the start of our friendship Prokofiev had said that he would like to rename one of the princesses in the story as a tribute to me. And so he did. The first princess, "Violetta," became "Linetta" in my honor.

At last, on December 30, 1921, the premiere was at hand. Prokofiev himself conducted. Public anticipation was great, and the Chicagoans were very proud. After the world premiere, THE LOVE FOR THREE ORANGES was presented on many stages, in many lands, and in many languages. The March and Scherzo from the opera became popular concert pieces and were recorded by the great orchestras of the world. Prokofiev transcribed them for the piano and performed them at his own recitals. Today's pianists still include them on their programs.

Recently, I attended a performance of THE LOVE FOR THREE ORANGES in Moscow, with several of my sons and grandchildren. We all liked the performance. I know that Sergei Sergeivitch would have enjoyed it.

Moscow, April 1965   LINA PROKOFIEV

King Sylvanus, ruler of the Kingdom of Clover, was terribly worried.

He had been a good king, he was popular and rich, and his people were happy. But all the same, he was terribly worried because suddenly in his old age, just when he wanted to hand over the reins of his kingdom to his handsome young son, Prince Tartaly, the Prince was always ill. One day he had violent headaches, the next he had pains in his back, then he had palpitations of the heart — and every time he went to sleep, he had nightmares.

Finally, in desperation, the King brought together the most distinguished medical specialists from the four corners of his empire to consult about the ailing Prince. The doctors took their turns at examining the boy. They poked his ribs, listened to his heart, and made him say "Ah" over and over again. Then they held a conference and declared that there was absolutely nothing wrong with the Prince: he was perfectly healthy. His illnesses were all imaginary, they said. Perhaps he had too much responsibility as a Prince. They sagely prescribed that he should be less a Prince and more an ordinary boy — and then his illnesses would vanish. In fact, the doctors chanted this slogan to help Prince Tartaly recover:

> "It's easy to tell
> What it takes to stay well:
> Only laughter can cure
> All the pains you endure."

"Make your son laugh," said the doctors to the King, "and he will be completely cured."

"But my son doesn't ever laugh," said the King. "Now that I think of it, I've *never* seen him laugh. But," he added, "if laughter will cure him, we shall certainly make him laugh. I know a very funny clown with a funny name; Truffaldino is bound to make Tartaly laugh." And turning to his Lord Chamberlain, he told him to send for Truffaldino and to arrange for circuses and festivals and feasts and balls and masquerades.

Having received the King's command, Truffaldino stayed up that whole night practicing tricks until they were absolutely perfect, and in the morning he painted his face all white, and his lips and nose a bright red, and put on his most outlandish costume. He went to the palace and crept into the Prince's room to take him by surprise. There was the Prince, sitting on his bed with a hot-water bottle on his head. All the tables and windowsills were covered with medicine bottles.

Suddenly Truffaldino began to sing:

"I'm Truffaldino the clown, ho, ho;
I'm a clown of renown, ho, ho.
Come watch as I wiggle my ears
And you'll laugh till your eyes fill
with tears."

As he jumped in the air and tumbled around the room, the Prince looked up sadly and said, "Go away, Truffaldino, you bore me. And besides, I have a terrible toothache." All day long Truffaldino jumped, juggled, and sang jingles to the pitiful Prince, but not once did the young boy even smile, let alone laugh. By evening Truffaldino was completely exhausted and left the palace, feeling as sad as the Prince.

The next day the festivals began in the market
place, and though Tartaly didn't want to get dressed
and certainly didn't want to go out in the hot mid-
day sun, his father's pleading was more than he
could bear, and he finally went to see the celebra-
tion. For hours he sat there watching trained horses

gallop and perform tricks, soldiers and sailors march
by to the music of colorful bands, and people from
the country villages perform dances in his honor.
Everyone in the Kingdom of Clover had a wonderful
time that day — except Tartaly, who complained of
the heat and the noise and kept begging his father
to let him go back to bed.

Finally, as the sun began to set, the King took pity on the boy and was just about to let him go back to the palace, when suddenly a great commotion arose in the square, just below the royal box. The King sent his guards to quiet the uproar and ordered them to bring the rowdy offenders up to him.

In a few moments the guards returned dragging an ugly old crone dressed in rags. She struggled so hard that when they let her go she slipped, turned a complete somersault in the air, and fell down right on her bustle. The scene was so funny that the Prince burst out laughing! What a happy moment that was for the King and all the people of the Kingdom of Clover! Soon everyone was laughing heartily — except the old lady herself. She knit her brow, waved her hands to the heavens — and in an instant, the market place was covered by a black, menacing cloud.

"Do you know who I am?" cried the old lady. "I am Fata Morgana."

"Fatty Morgana," shouted the Prince and started laughing all over again.

But the shrew waved her hands in the air again, and the skies cracked with thunder, and sharp streaks of lightning shot down into the square. "I'm Fata Morgana," she shouted, "the Evil Witch."

"Ohhhhhhhhhh," moaned the Prince, and "Ohhh-hhhhhh," moaned everyone else in the square, because they had all heard of the Evil Witch, though they hadn't known her name. They did know that she had great magical power and could do much harm.

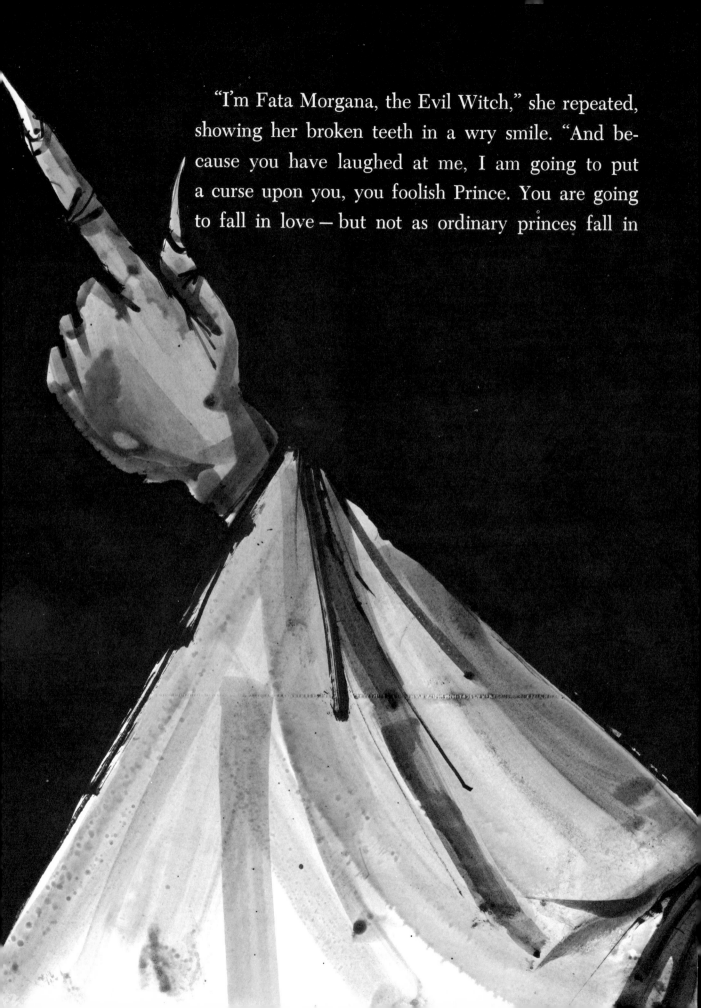

"I'm Fata Morgana, the Evil Witch," she repeated, showing her broken teeth in a wry smile. "And because you have laughed at me, I am going to put a curse upon you, you foolish Prince. You are going to fall in love — but not as ordinary princes fall in

love. Instead of falling in love with a princess, you will fall in love with three oranges. That's right, three oranges. And you must ride three thousand miles to reach them. You will not be happy, ever, until you find them. There! That will teach you to laugh at Fata Morgana." And in a flash of lightning, she vanished.

The young Prince shook his head as if awakening from a dream, and the first words he uttered were "three oranges."

"I must find the three oranges, and I know where to find them if they are three thousand miles away: they must be with Creonta the giantess. Quick, guards, get me my armor, my sword, and my helmet. Get my horses ready. And Truffaldino, you will go with me. Come on, let's hurry," and he began to sing:

"I'm in love with oranges three,
And I'll find them, just wait and see."

Everyone shuddered when the Prince mentioned Creonta, because travelers had brought back hair-raising stories about this horrible creature who ruled over the Kingdom of Doom. The King pleaded with Tartaly not to go, but the Prince was adamant:

"I'm in love with oranges three,
    And I'll find them, just wait and see.
    Happy I can never be
    Till I find my oranges three."

"Very well, then," said the King, "but I shall send the court magician, Celio, to look after you." And off the Prince and Truffaldino went in search of the Kingdom of Doom.

They traveled far and wide, by land and by sea,
by day and by night,

until they saw the big black
mountains that surrounded Creonta's dark kingdom.

Truffaldino was very tired and very frightened when he saw those mountains, but the Prince cheered him up and promised to protect him. "Besides," said the Prince, "the magician Celio will look after us and won't let anyone hurt us, not even big, ugly Creonta. Helloooooooo, Celio; are you there, Celio; come and tell Truffaldino that there's nothing to worry about." And out of a rock by the side of the road came a puff of smoke, and there beside them stood a smiling man with a wand in his hand.

"Certainly," said Celio, "I shall look after you. But you must be careful. Creonta is not just an ordinary giantess; she's clever and strong. She likes to cook, you know, and she can cook up the most deadly poisons in the world. Don't eat or drink a thing while you're in the Kingdom of Doom."

"Very well," said the Prince, "we won't."

"And remember," added Celio, "if you find the three oranges, don't cut them open without some water handy. Now I must leave you, but here's a magic ribbon that will probably be useful." And he disappeared in another puff of smoke.

"See, Truffaldino, we have nothing to worry about, especially with this magic ribbon. Now let's hurry to the other side of those mountains and find the three oranges." And although Truffaldino was not entirely convinced, they galloped off toward the Kingdom of Doom.

They crossed the black mountains and came to Creonta's big, gloomy castle. As they stood looking at the monstrous building, one of the huge doors started creaking, and out came an ugly hag about ten feet tall, wearing a dirty apron around her huge waist and waving spoons and ladles with both hands. Truffaldino's knees started shaking and he said to the Prince: "Please, Your Highness, keep that magic ribbon ready." The Prince was by now a little frightened too, and he felt in his breast pocket to make sure that the ribbon was still there.

"Ahhhhhhhhhh," cried Creonta, "I smell a mouse or two. Stop trying to hide in the corner there. You can't hide from Creonta. I see you, you niggling little beasts." And dropping her spoons and ladles, she picked up the Prince in her right hand and Truffaldino in her left.

Looking at Truffaldino twisting and squirming, she said, "Hmmmmmmmm, I think I'll fry you; you would go well smothered in butter with a piece of parsley as a garnish. And you," she said as she turned to the Prince, "you look as though you'd taste best marinated. Yes, I shall marinate you." And she laughed at the top of her loud voice.

In desperation the Prince pulled out the red ribbon that Celio had given him and held it up for Creonta to see. "Creonta," he shouted, "this is a magic ribbon, and you can have it if you let us go."

"Magic ribbon? What do you mean, magic ribbon? What magic does it do?"

"Well, it makes people beautiful. Just put it on and see."

"You don't say," said Creonta. "It is a lovely silk ribbon, isn't it?" she observed as the Prince gave it to her. "You say it makes girls beautiful? Oh, I simply must try it." And, putting the Prince and Truffaldino down, off she went to look for a mirror so that she could tie the ribbon in her hair, singing as she went:
"I'm rather a plain-looking girl, I know;
But perhaps I'll look better with this silken bow.
Oh, for a mirror; oh, for a glass;
Oh, to become a pretty lass."

As soon as Creonta was out of sight, the Prince said to Truffaldino: "You wait here. I'm going into the palace kitchen to look for the three oranges." He found the kitchen easily enough because the palace was filled with cooking odors that led him right to their source. And once in the kitchen, it was easy to find the pantry. There, at one end of the room, in a cardboard box lay three huge oranges. They were so big that the Prince had to cradle his arms to carry them out of the palace.

"Quick, Truffaldino," said the Prince, struggling under the weight of the oranges, "let's start for home immediately, before Creonta comes back." And off they went, over the mountains and into the desert before Creonta could catch them.

But the trip across the desert was long and tiring, and they were burdened by the extra weight of the oranges, which seemed to grow bigger and heavier every day. Soon they ran out of the water they had brought with them from the Kingdom of Clover, and they grew thirstier and thirstier. Then, one night as they lay sleeping on the desert, Truffaldino suddenly awoke with a desperate thirst.

"Oh, I wish I weren't so thirsty," he said, "because I know that I mustn't eat the oranges. But I am so very thirsty, and the oranges must be so very juicy, so thirst-quenching, so cool and refreshing from the night air." Unable to resist temptation any longer, he bit into one of the oranges.

But as he did so, the orange fell away and there before him stood a beautiful young girl dressed in a white satin gown. "Who are you?" she asked. "For I am Princess Linetta."

"Oh," groaned Truffaldino, thinking only of his thirst, "I wish you were a glass of orange juice."

"Where is the water you are supposed to have for me?" asked the Princess. "Didn't Celio tell you that I must have some water, at least a drop? If you don't give me some water to drink in the next few seconds, I shall disappear."

"Oh, don't disappear," cried Truffaldino. "Here are two other oranges. Let's cut one open and we can both have some juice to quench our thirst," and he tried to cut open the second orange. But the same thing happened: another flash of light, and there was another beautiful young Princess.

"My name is Nicoletta," she said. "Where is the water you're supposed to have waiting for me to drink?"

"Oh me," cried Truffaldino, "this is hopeless," and he started crying so loud and disagreeably that he woke up the Prince. But by the time the Prince was awakened, both Princesses had disappeared.

Seeing only one orange left, the Prince was certain that the three oranges had miraculously become one, and he was sure that the orange contained the object of his love. He cut it open — and there before him stood a lovely Princess.

"My name is Ninetta," she said. "Where is the water I must drink if I am not to vanish?"

"Oh, my lovely Ninetta," the Prince said, "I have been searching for you all over the world. You are my only love. How happy I am to find you!"

"And I love you too, dear Prince Tartaly, but if you don't give me some water to drink in the next few seconds, I shall disappear. Quick! I am growing weak, my head is beginning to spin, I am beginning to fade away. . . . Oh . . ."

Fortunately Celio had been observing the Prince's dilemma, and in a flash he appeared with a bucket of water. Instantly the Prince gave some to his lovely Ninetta and she revived.

"Thank you, dear Prince," she said, "you have saved my life, and I shall be ever grateful to you."

"And now," said the Prince, "we must go to see my father, King of Clover."

"Oh, no," cried Ninetta, "not in this dress. It's stained with orange juice. You must first bring me something more appropriate to wear when I meet the King."

"Very well," said the Prince, "I shall go home and bring you the most beautiful gown in the whole Kingdom." And off he went.

The Princess was very tired from having been trapped in the orange for so long, and she lay down on the desert sands to sleep. But just as soon as she fell asleep, Fata Morgana and her servant, Smeraldina, came crawling up. Out of her rags, Fata Morgana pulled a long needle, and with it she drew the picture of a rat in the sand. Then she plunged her magic needle into the picture, and the Princess suddenly turned into a huge rat and went scampering off into the desert.

Fata Morgana laughed and turning to her servant she said, "Smeraldina, you must lie down here and make believe you are asleep. When the Prince returns, he will think you are Princess Ninetta and marry you. Then, one day you will be Queen of Clover."

In the meantime, the Prince had returned to his palace, ordered beautiful dresses to be prepared, and set out once again for the desert, this time with his father, the King, and a large contingent of royalty.

Before long, they found the spot where the Prince had left Ninetta, but when he saw Smeraldina, all his excitement fled.

"You are not Princess Ninetta," cried the Prince indignantly.

"Yes, I am," said Smeraldina, "Oh, how terrible, the Prince doesn't love me any more!"

"Excuse my son, Princess," said the King, intervening in the argument. "He does not have a very good memory, and he is obviously bad-mannered. Since he's given his word to marry you, however, I shall see to it that he does."

The King then ordered everyone to return to the palace, and when they all arrived there, he asked his lords and ladies to dress up in their finest robes and assemble in the throne room for the Prince's wedding to Princess Ninetta.

At the appointed hour the heralds sounded their trumpets and all the guests gathered before the carved doors of the throne room. The King was the first to enter, and all the guests followed. But imagine their surprise when on the throne meant for the new Princess they saw a huge desert rat. The King was shocked and grew angry, and he ordered the guards to remove the rat. But at that moment a puff of smoke rose from behind the jeweled throne, and there stood the court magician, Celio.

"Forgive this intrusion, dear King," he said, "but Fata Morgana, the Evil Witch, has beguiled you. The woman by the Prince's side is not Princess Ninetta; she is Smeraldina, Fata Morgana's servant. The real Princess Ninetta is here, Your Majesty," and he pointed to the huge rat, "made to appear so unpleasant by the Evil Witch herself."

He waved his wand over the rat, which immediately turned into the real Princess. The Prince, overjoyed, rushed up to her, and shouted, "See, Father, this is my Ninetta, the one I really love."

The King ordered Smeraldina turned out of the palace, thanked Celio for his great service to the Kingdom, and declared that the wedding would take place as quickly as Princess Ninetta could change from her juice-stained dress into a proper wedding gown.

That evening the young couple were married, and for weeks thereafter all the people of the Kingdom of Clover danced in the streets. The young Prince appointed Truffaldino Official Clown to the Court, and to mark the end of his years of illness, he ordered all the medicine bottles in his room replaced by singing birds and sweet-smelling flowers. Everyone was happy, and laughter rang through the halls of the palace.

About John Moreton

JOHN MORETON might be described as an author, educator, and full-time opera buff. A native of Calgary, Canada, Mr. Moreton was educated in the U.S. and received his Ph.D. at Columbia University, New York. In addition to his duties as Associate Professor of English at New York's City College and Syracuse University, the author is at present editing the Lewis Carroll letters on a Guggenheim fellowship and has also published studies on H. Rider Haggard and Rudyard Kipling. His first book for children was PUNKY: MOUSE FOR A DAY, published by Putnam's and a Junior Literary Guild selection.

About Murray Tinkelman

MURRAY TINKELMAN was born and raised in New York. A graduate of Cooper Union, he has exhibited in both one-man and group shows, in museums and galleries throughout the country, including the Denver Art Museum, the De Cordova Museum in Boston, the Brooklyn Museum, and the New York City Center Art Gallery. His work is presently included in the permanent collections at the University of Minnesota and the Brooklyn Museum. Mr. Tinkelman's picture books have been frequently included in yearly exhibits of outstanding book illustration by the AIGA and the Society of Illustrators. In addition to illustrating for such national magazines as *American Heritage* and *Harper's Bazaar,* the artist also teaches at the Parsons School of Design. He collaborated previously with John Moreton to produce PUNKY: MOUSE FOR A DAY, and with Eve Merriam on DON'T THINK ABOUT A WHITE BEAR, both for Putnam's.

Contents

Getting the most from this book

This *Need to Know* guide is designed to help you throughout your course as a companion to your learning and a revision aid in the months or weeks leading up to the final exams.

The following features in each section will help you get the most from the book.

You need to know

Each topic begins with a list summarising what you 'need to know' in this topic for the exam.

Exam tip

Key knowledge you need to demonstrate in the exam, tips on exam technique, common misconceptions to avoid and important things to remember.

Key terms

Definitions of highlighted terms in the text to make sure you know the essential terminology for your subject.

Do you know?

Questions at the end of each topic to test you on some of its key points. Check your answers here: www.hoddereducation.co.uk/needtoknow/answers

Synoptic links

Reminders of how knowledge and skills from different topics in your A-level relate to one another.

End of section questions

Questions at the end of each main section of the book to test your knowledge of the specification area covered. Check your answers here: www.hoddereducation.co.uk/needtoknow/answers

NEED to KNOW

AQA A-LEVEL COMPUTER SCIENCE

Stuart Davison

HODDER EDUCATION
AN HACHETTE UK COMPANY

Hachette UK's policy is to use papers that are natural, renewable and recyclable products and made from wood grown in sustainable forests. The logging and manufacturing processes are expected to conform to the environmental regulations of the country of origin.

Orders: please contact Bookpoint Ltd, 130 Park Drive, Milton Park, Abingdon, Oxon OX14 4SE. Telephone: (44) 01235 827827. Fax: (44) 01235 400401. Email: education@bookpoint.co.uk

Lines are open from 9 a.m. to 5 p.m., Monday to Saturday, with a 24-hour message answering service. You can also order through our website: www.hoddereducation.co.uk

ISBN: 978 1 5104 2856 0

First published in 2018 by

Hodder Education,
An Hachette UK Company
Carmelite House
50 Victoria Embankment
London EC4Y 0DZ

Impression number   10 9 8 7 6 5 4 3 2 1

Year   2022 2021 2020 2019 2018

Typeset in India by Aptara

Printed in Spain

A catalogue record for this title is available from the British Library.

MIX
Paper from
responsible sources
FSC™ C104740

① Programming and computation

1.1 Fundamentals of programming

You need to know

- Programs utilise three principal statements.
- Values are stored in constants and variables.
- Data is categorised by type.
- Operators act on values to produce results.
- A string is an object data type with specific handling operations.
- Exception handling catches errors.
- Subroutines are blocks of code that perform tasks.
- Object-oriented programming encapsulates data within objects.

Programming

Programming concepts

There are three principal statements used in all **imperative programming** languages.

- Sequence: a completed action triggers the next action in a predetermined order.
- Selection: the flow of a program is changed based on the answer to a condition.
- Iteration: repeated passes through a group of instructions.

The repetition of instructions can be:
- definite: the number of loops is known before the loop starts
- indefinite: the loop continues until a stopping condition is realised

Where a condition stops a loop, it can be placed either at the beginning of the loop or at the end.

Key term

Imperative programming
Languages that describe the sequence of instructions to follow in order to change the state of a program.

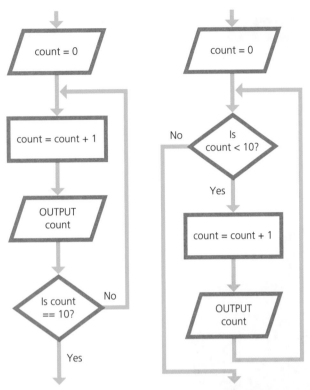

Figure 1 Conditions that end loops can either be at the top or bottom of the loop. Both these loops output the numbers 1 to 10

Other important programming concepts:
- selection and iteration can be **nested** inside other similar statements to complete before finishing the initial statement
- programs also need to include declarations of variables and constants in addition to any definitions of subroutines

Constants and variables

Computer programs make use of values to produce useful outputs.

These value stored can be stored in named locations known as:
- variables: value stored can be changed as the program runs
- constants: value stored is kept the same throughout the lifetime of the program

Constants are used where important values need to be kept the same throughout a program, for example, pi is set to 3.14 and will never need to be changed.

Data types

Data types are applied to values to determine the format that the values can take and the operations that can be performed on them. Variables and constants are declared with a data type so that appropriate values can be stored and used appropriately.

Table 1 Common data types

Term	Definition
Integer	Whole numbers
Real/float	Numbers with a fractional part
Boolean	Either true or false
Character	Single alphanumeric character
String	A collection of characters as an object
Date/time	Pre-formatted to express dates and times correctly
Pointer	Address of a memory location
Record	Grouped collection of a number of variables
Array	Collection of values each with the same data type

> **Exam tip**
>
> Make sure you are aware of the uses of different data types within typical computer programs. You should be able to select the most appropriate data type for a given scenario.

Operators

Operators work with values to produce a result.

Arithmetic operators perform mathematical operations.

- Addition: 2 + 2 evaluates to 4.
- Subtraction: 5 − 3 evaluates to 2.
- Multiplication: 5 × 8 evaluates to 40.
- Integer division: provides just the whole number part of a division so 7 DIV 3 evaluates to 2.
- Remainder division: provides only the remainder part of the division so 7 MOD 3 evaluates to 1.
- Real/float division: provides the result of the division as a decimal so 7/2 evaluates to 3.5.
- Exponential: raises a value to a power so 2 ^ 3 evaluates to 8.
- Rounding: changes values to the nearest whole number so round(7.6) evaluates to 8.
- Truncating: removes unrequired parts of a value so trunc(7.6) evaluates to 7 (note that casting a real value as an integer can also have the same effect, e.g. int(7.6) produces the value 7).

> **Key terms**
>
> **Arithmetic operator** Takes values called operands and performs a mathematical operation on them to produce a result.
>
> **Relational operator** Compares two values to determine the way they differ or if they are the same.

Operators that compare values

The **relational operators** used in programming are:
- equal to: checks two values are the same so 3 = 2 evaluates to False
- not equal to: checks two values are different so 3 <> 2 evaluates to True
- less than: 5 < 3 evaluates to False
- greater than: 4 > 0 evaluates to True
- less than or equal to: 7 <= 9 evaluates to True
- greater than or equal to: 5 >= 2 evaluates to True

Results from relational operations are commonly used to provide control over selection and iteration statements. The result of these comparisons is either a True or False Boolean value.

There are four common **Boolean operators**:

- AND: joining expressions both need to be True to give a True result so 5 > 3 AND 4 < 6 evaluates to True
- OR: only one joining expression needs to be True to give a True result so 4 > 10 OR 3 < 4 evaluates to True
- NOT: inverts the result of a relational expression so NOT 5 > 0 evaluates to False
- XOR: only one joining expression can be True to give a True result so 7 > 1 XOR 8 < 9 evaluates to False

> **Key term**
>
> **Boolean operator** Used to combine statements that use relational operators.

String handling

A string is a combination of a variable number of character values treated as its own data type together with operations that can be used to summarise its properties.

Table 2 **Common string-handling operations**

Operation	Description
Length	The number of characters in the string, e.g. LEN("hello") evaluates to 5
Position	Finds the first position of a given character, e.g. POSITION("hello", "e") evaluates to 1 (the first position in a string is 0)
Substring	Returns a requested part of a string, e.g. SUBSTRING(2, 4, "hello") evaluates to "llo"
Concatenation	Joins strings together, e.g. "hel" + "lo" evaluates to "hello"
Character to character code	Determines the equivalent ASCII code for a specified character, e.g. CHAR_TO_CODE("s") evaluates to 83
Character code to character	Determines the character from a given ASCII code, e.g. CODE_TO_CHAR(68) evaluates to "d"

String conversion operations translate string values to other data types and back again if required.

> **Synoptic link**
>
> The representation of a data value as a numerical (and ultimately binary) value such as an ASCII code is considered in greater detail in Section 2.1.

Random number generation

Key points:

- Sometimes values that have not been inputted or calculated are needed in a program.
- Random number generation is a feature in programming languages that produces a value between a given range.

For example, if a random integer between the range 0 and 9 was required, the random function would need to be called with these values.

The result would be assigned to a variable as follows:

```
randDigit = RANDOM_INT(0, 9)
```

Exception handling

Key points:

- **Exceptions** in programs are errors that cause it to stop working, rendering it unusable.
- Code can be written to take action when exceptions are detected.
- An alternative block of code can run to ensure the remainder of the program executes normally.

This is an example of exception handling in Python that prevents characters being entered when an integer is expected:

```
try:
    score = int(input("Enter your test score: "))
except:
    print("Not a number. Score set to zero.")
    score = 0
print("Your test percentage was:"(score/50)×100)
```

Subroutines

Subroutines:

- are units of code that are 'out of line' of the main program and are called to run to produce repeatable results
- can be run from any point in a program using the name of the subroutine, any number of times, e.g. `displayTemperature()`
- make code easier to read as repeated blocks of code are replaced by a single identifier
- save development time as code does not have to be repeated
- allow changes to be made in a single location

Values in and out of subroutines

Key points:

- Data is passed from the calling program to a subroutine using a **parameter**.
- A result from a subroutine can be passed back to the calling program using a **return value**.
- This boundary in and out of the subroutine is known as its interface.

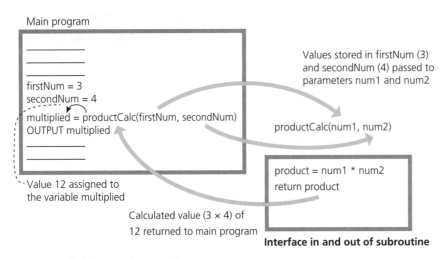

Main program

firstNum = 3
secondNum = 4
multiplied = productCalc(firstNum, secondNum)
OUTPUT multiplied

Value 12 assigned to
the variable multiplied

Values stored in firstNum (3)
and secondNum (4) passed to
parameters num1 and num2

productCalc(num1, num2)

product = num1 * num2
return product

Calculated value (3 × 4) of
12 returned to main program

Interface in and out of subroutine

Figure 2 Values can be
passed as parameters into a
subroutine for use. Any result
can be passed back as a return
value

Data within subroutines

Key points:

- Any variable created inside a subroutine is referred as a **local variable** and can only be accessed by instructions internal to the subroutine.
- Once the subroutine has finished, these values cease to exist.
- Variables that subroutines use can be either **global** or **local** in **scope**.
- It is good practice to try and limit variable creation to local scope and pass any data in and out of a subroutine using its interface.
- This ensures that the places to change values in a program are limited compared to global scope variables which can be changed anywhere.

Stack frames in subroutine calls

Key points:

- In computer memory, the state of different program subroutines is stored in a **call stack** as a collection of **stack frames**.
- The stack builds from the bottom up.
- As a subroutine is called it is pushed on to the top of the stack.
- When the subroutine finishes, it is popped back off the stack and the previous program continues to run.

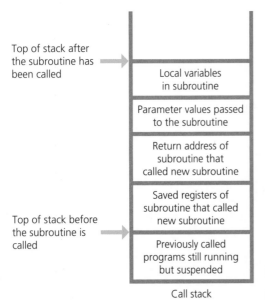

Top of stack after
the subroutine has
been called

Local variables
in subroutine

Parameter values passed
to the subroutine

Return address of
subroutine that
called new subroutine

Saved registers of
subroutine that called
new subroutine

Top of stack before
the subroutine is
called

Previously called
programs still running
but suspended

Call stack

**Figure 3 Stack frame
arrangement**

Key terms

Local variables are created
inside a subroutine and are
usable only by code in that
same subroutine.

Global variables are created
outside of any subroutine
and can be changed
anywhere in a program.

Scope The extent to which
variables are visible.

Call stack A data
structure that is used to
store information about
subroutines running as part
of a computer program.

Stack frame The collection
of data that describes the
current running state of a
program.

Synoptic link

Effective design of
programs lends itself to
the decomposition of
a problem into several
smaller solutions that
can be implemented as
subroutines. See Section 2.9
for more information about
software design.

Stack frames are created as follows.

1. When a program calls a subroutine to run, the state of the current program is saved.
2. The memory address of where any return value should be copied is added.
3. Values passed into the subroutine are stored.
4. Local subroutine variables are added.

Recursive techniques

Key points:

- As subroutines are stored in a stack, the results from them can be delayed until other subroutines finish.
- The result of one subroutine can be used as a parameter for another copy of the same subroutine.
- Further subroutines are called until a base case is reached.
- The base case stops any other subroutine calls and the results are passed back to all waiting subroutines.
- This chain is known as **recursion**.

Programming paradigms

Procedural programming enforces the use of subroutines to provide highly structured code.

Object-oriented programming groups data and instructions together as objects that interact with each other in a tightly controlled manner.

Procedural programming

Key features of procedural programming:

- Key functions are sectioned off into subroutines referred to as procedures.
- Each procedure performs a specific task and is called, in turn, by a main program.
- Structured procedural programs can be designed using hierarchy charts.

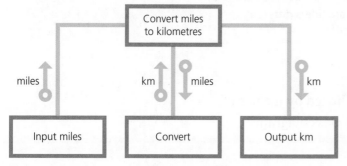

Figure 4 **Designing a program that uses subroutines with a hierarchy chart**

Synoptic link

Stacks and other data structures are discussed in more detail in Section 1.2.

Key terms

Recursion A method of repeating program code by calling copies of the same program until an end condition is reached.

Programming paradigm The approach of writing programs, each requiring different techniques.

Exam tip

Understanding recursion requires practice. Functional programs, as described in Section 2.8, are based around this concept and provide a means of appreciating how this technique works.

Structured design is advantageous because:

■ code is easier to read and change
■ procedures can be reused
■ small parts can be tested and, once working, can be left to function without affecting other parts of the code

Object-oriented programming

Programmers use **object-oriented** methods to create scalable programs with the advantages of:
■ producing easily reusable code
■ hiding data within objects to protect it from uncontrolled modification
■ as programs get bigger, object-oriented designs become more manageable
■ components are easier to maintain

Object-oriented programming utilises the design concepts in Table 3.

Table 3 Design concepts

Concept	Definition
Class	Defines the data that characterises the object described (attributes) and the behaviours the object has (methods)
Object	Created from the class using a constructor
Instantiation	The act of creating objects from the class definition
Encapsulation	The act of collecting data within an object, often hidden from public view
Inheritance	Where new objects or classes take on properties of existing ones
Aggregation	The relationship of objects where the destruction of the owning object does not destroy associated objects
Composition	An association of objects where the destruction of a parent object results in related objects also being destroyed
Polymorphism	Where inherited objects retain named methods of parent classes but with the option to adjust the behaviour accordingly
Overriding	The opportunity for subclasses to provide a different implementation of a parent method

Class diagrams

The design of object-oriented programs is facilitated by the use of standardised **Unified Modelling Language (UML)** class diagrams.

1 Classes named in bold.
2 Public attributes (+) changeable by anything.
3 Private attributes (−) changeable only within the class.

Key terms

Object-oriented programming Programs are designed and created as a series of objects that store data and provide controls to access and modify this data.

Unified Modelling Language (UML) A standardised set of approaches used to specify and describe the behaviours and operation of a system.

4 Protected attributes (#) changeable in own class and other related classes.

5 Public method (+) called by anything to perform action on object.

6 Class inherited by parent (where arrow points) taking on its properties and methods.

7 Composition relating objects from another class. If the parent is destroyed, so is the child.

8 Aggregation relating objects in a way that doesn't destroy the child when the parent is destroyed.

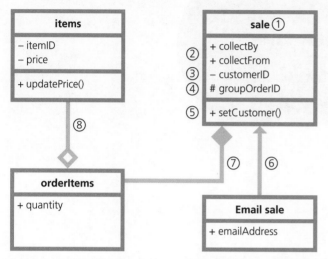

Figure 5 Features of a UML standard object-oriented program design

Do you know?

1 What are the three principal programming statements that all imperative programs are built from?

2 In some programming languages, data values are stored using variables that have been assigned a type. What is a data type?

3 What can be used on operand values to produce new values?

4 What are strings?

5 Subroutines are separate units of code away from a main program. How can data be transferred in and out of a subroutine?

6 An object-oriented school timetable program contains objects made from a pupil class and a lesson class. How should these classes be associated? Give a reason for your answer.

1.2 Fundamentals of data structures

You need to know

- Data structures are built from fundamental data types.
- Arrays and records are common data structures.
- Files are used to store data outside of programs.
- Abstract data types (ADTs) are models for organising data.
- Abstract data types are realised using data structures.
- Queues, stacks, graphs, trees, hash tables, dictionaries and vectors are common ADTs.

Data structures and abstract types

Data structures

Key points:
- Data in computer programs can be organised into different structures.
- The choice of structure is dependent on the way the data will be processed.
- Data structures are built from the fundamental data types available in the programming language to create more complex arrangements.

Synoptic link

See Section 1.1 for more details about the fundamental data types in computer programming.

Arrays

Key points:
- Collections of values stored are **array** elements.
- Access to the different elements is controlled by an index value that is changed by the same amount based on the data type used.
- Arrays can use additional index values to allow more complex sets of data to be stored.

Key term

Array A data structure that is a continuous collection of variables all of the same data type.

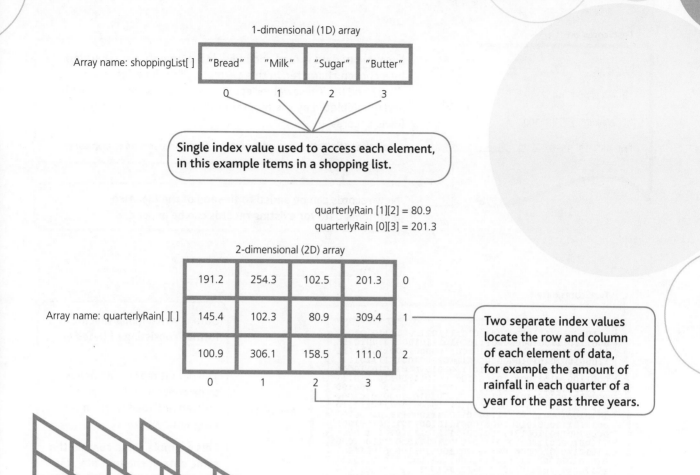

1-dimensional (1D) array

Array name: shoppingList[ ]

"Bread"	"Milk"	"Sugar"	"Butter"
0	1	2	3

Single index value used to access each element, in this example items in a shopping list.

quarterlyRain [1][2] = 80.9
quarterlyRain [0][3] = 201.3

2-dimensional (2D) array

Array name: quarterlyRain[ ][ ]

191.2	254.3	102.5	201.3	0
145.4	102.3	80.9	309.4	1
100.9	306.1	158.5	111.0	2
0	1	2	3	

Two separate index values locate the row and column of each element of data, for example the amount of rainfall in each quarter of a year for the past three years.

Arrays can be constructed using as many dimensions as required (*n*-dimensional arrays where *n* is the number of index values used to reference each data element).

Figure 6 Arrays with different dimensions

Fields, records and files

When a program terminates, all the data it holds is lost unless a file is used. Programs need to be able to store and retrieve data to and from files if they are to make use of this data.

Data can be encoded within files as different formats.

- Text files: data is stored as a series of readable alphanumeric characters that don't require additional conversion to make them usable.
- Binary files: data is stored as sequence of bytes understandable by the programs that interact with the data.

TestScores.txt

"J. Smith", 75, 67, 89

"B. Jones", 22, 44, 73

"T. Walker", 47, 88, 100

"M. Ali", 13, 96, 57

Text file

Each line of data is read and individual elements are separated by a chosen character. In this example, J Smith had test scores of 75, 67 and 89. These values could be stored in separate variables and manipulated by the program to find averages and highest and lowest scores.

Note that the data is read from the file and used as it appears.

New records can be added to the end of the file. Also, additional data for existing records can be appended.

TestScores.data

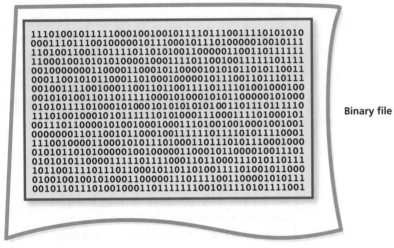

Binary file

Data is written in a specific format consisting of bytes of data.

The data it represents needs to be converted when being written and read to/from the program.

This example could contain the same data as the text file, it is just represented in a different way.

Figure 7 Comparison of text and binary files

Abstract data types and data structures

Common ADTs include:

- queues
- stacks
- graphs
- trees
- hash tables
- dictionaries
- vectors

Static versus dynamic

The underlying data structures that implement these types can be either static or dynamic.

- Static: the size of the structure is fixed and cannot be changed when the program is running.
- Dynamic: the size of the structure varies as the data changes during the execution of the program.

Key terms

Data file A computer file where data is stored from a running program for use in future executions.

Abstract data types (ADTs) Models of data constructed within computer programs, organised by how the data will be processed.

Table 4 Advantages and disadvantages of static and dynamic data structures

	Static	Dynamic
Flexibility	Fixed amount of data elements that cannot be changed, limiting flexibility of the structure.	Can adjust the number of data elements stored within the structure as required.
Access	Fixed size allows an efficient allocation within memory. This results in quicker access to elements.	The flexible nature of the structure means that access to specific elements takes longer.
Size of structure	As the number of elements is fixed there is the potential for unused space being allocated to the structure.	Elements are only added when needed, ensuring that the data structure is kept as small as required.

> ### Exam tip
>
> As well as knowing the properties and features of ADTs, you should be aware of how they are used by programmers to store and retrieve data effectively. Different ADTs allow more efficient processing under different operating conditions.

Queues

Key points:

- A collection of data where the order in which elements are added is the order in which they are processed.
- The data at the front of the queue is processed first.
- New data is added to the rear of the queue.
- Queues can be implemented in a variety of ways.

Example: queue implementations

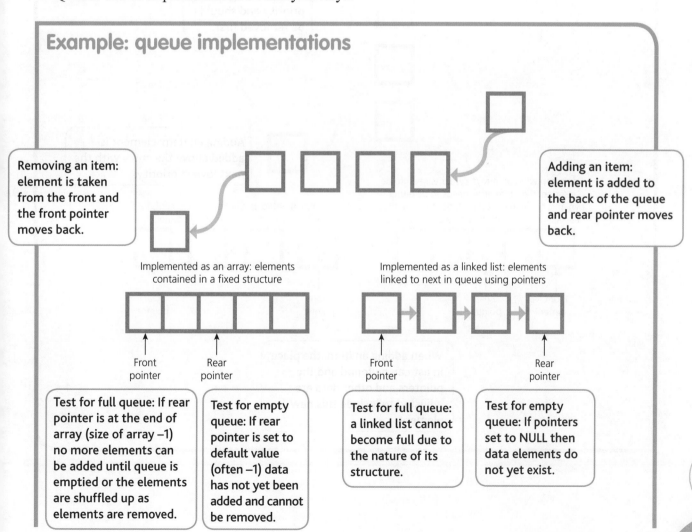

Removing an item: element is taken from the front and the front pointer moves back.

Adding an item: element is added to the back of the queue and rear pointer moves back.

Implemented as an array: elements contained in a fixed structure

Implemented as a linked list: elements linked to next in queue using pointers

Front pointer — Rear pointer

Front pointer — Rear pointer

Test for full queue: If rear pointer is at the end of array (size of array −1) no more elements can be added until queue is emptied or the elements are shuffled up as elements are removed.

Test for empty queue: If rear pointer is set to default value (often −1) data has not yet been added and cannot be removed.

Test for full queue: a linked list cannot become full due to the nature of its structure.

Test for empty queue: If pointers set to NULL then data elements do not yet exist.

Removing an item: element is taken from the front and the front pointer moves towards the rear pointer.

Adding an item: element is added to the back of the queue and rear pointer moves away from the front pointer.

Implemented as an array: elements contained in a fixed structure, but this time can wrap around the ends

Front pointer

Rear pointer

Implemented as a linked list: elements linked to next in queue using pointers and looped back to start

Front pointer

Rear pointer

Test for full queue: If front pointer is one ahead of the rear pointer, the queue has become full.

Removing an item: element at front of queue has highest priority and should be removed first.

Adding an item: element is added above the entry with the next lowest priority.

Implemented as an array: elements need to be inserted, therefore array needs to be either dynamic or a large enough static structure that allows movement of data between elements

Front pointer

Rear pointer

Implemented as a linked list: elements linked to next in queue using pointers

Front pointer

Rear pointer

When adding an item, the place in list can be found and the pointers and other data are adjusted to include this new element.

Stacks

Key points:

- A collection of data where items that are added last are the first to be processed.
- Data is stored on a stack by being pushed on.
- When data is removed from the stack it is popped off.

Example: stack implementations

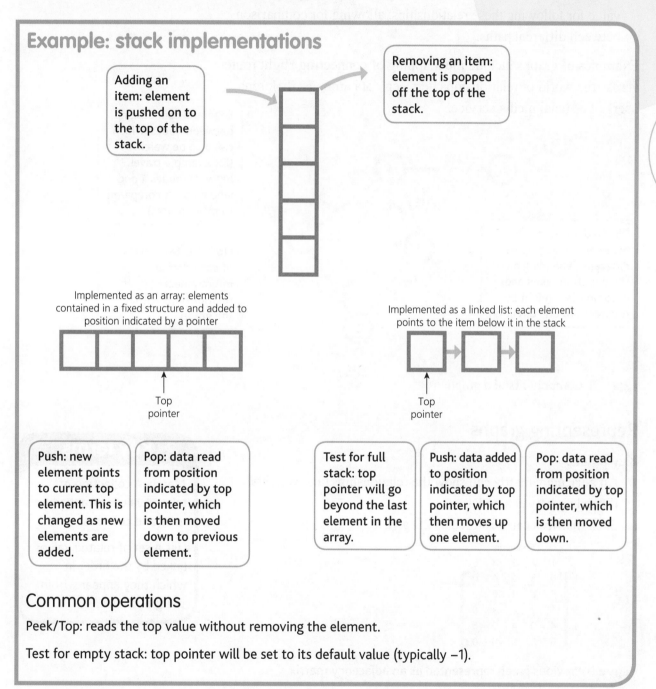

Adding an item: element is pushed on to the top of the stack.

Removing an item: element is popped off the top of the stack.

Implemented as an array: elements contained in a fixed structure and added to position indicated by a pointer

Top pointer

Implemented as a linked list: each element points to the item below it in the stack

Top pointer

Push: new element points to current top element. This is changed as new elements are added.

Pop: data read from position indicated by top pointer, which is then moved down to previous element.

Test for full stack: top pointer will go beyond the last element in the array.

Push: data added to position indicated by top pointer, which then moves up one element.

Pop: data read from position indicated by top pointer, which is then moved down.

Common operations

Peek/Top: reads the top value without removing the element.

Test for empty stack: top pointer will be set to its default value (typically −1).

Graphs

Key points:

■ Suitable for collections where the data has complex relationships.

■ A standard graph is used to show the relationships between sets of data.

■ Weighted graphs expand on standard graphs by assigning a value for following these relationships, allowing for comparison between different paths.

Examples of graphs include the mapping of connecting flight routes across the world or relationships between data amongst different users of a social media service.

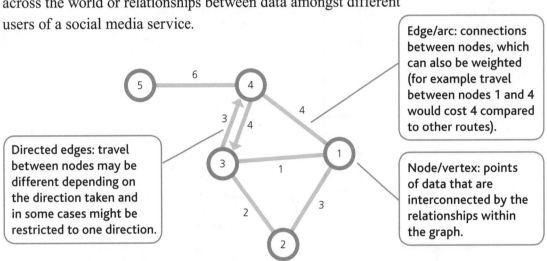

Edge/arc: connections between nodes, which can also be weighted (for example travel between nodes 1 and 4 would cost 4 compared to other routes).

Directed edges: travel between nodes may be different depending on the direction taken and in some cases might be restricted to one direction.

Node/vertex: points of data that are interconnected by the relationships within the graph.

Figure 8 Components of a graph

Representing graphs

Key points:

■ An adjacency **matrix** can show the relationships (and weights, if needed) between nodes.

■ Such matrices can be stored as 2D arrays.

	End node				
	1	2	3	4	5
1	0	3	1	4	0
2	3	0	2	0	0
Start node 3	1	2	0	3	0
4	4	0	4	0	6
5	0	0	0	6	0

Figure 9 Previous graph represented as an adjacency matrix

■ An adjacency **list** can be used as an alternative, where each starting node has its own list showing which other nodes are directly connected to it.

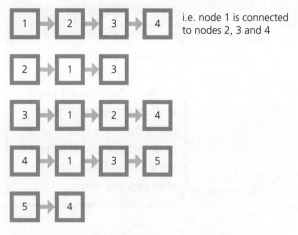

i.e. node 1 is connected
to nodes 2, 3 and 4

Figure 10 Previous graph as an adjacency list

- When a graph is sparsely populated (few connections between nodes) an adjacency matrix contains more unused elements than an adjacency list.
- Adjacency lists that have more than one connection per node can take longer to test if nodes are connected, as the whole list needs to be traversed.

Trees

Key points:
- A form of graph where the nodes are undirected and connected without any circular paths.
- Trees can also be formed as rooted trees in which one node is designated as the root.

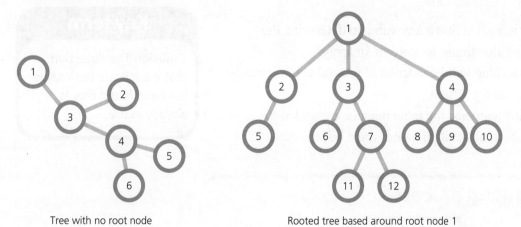

Tree with no root node   Rooted tree based around root node 1

Figure 11 Specific forms of binary trees

- A binary tree is a rooted tree where each node has, at most, connections to two other child nodes.
- Rooted trees are useful as data is encountered using the first node as a reference point.
- Retrieval routines traverse the tree to find order in the data.

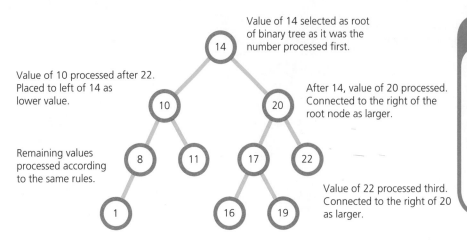

Value of 14 selected as root of binary tree as it was the number processed first.

Value of 10 processed after 22. Placed to left of 14 as lower value.

After 14, value of 20 processed. Connected to the right of the root node as larger.

Remaining values processed according to the same rules.

Value of 22 processed third. Connected to the right of 20 as larger.

Figure 12 Binary tree

Hash tables

Key points:

- Keys are created for series of values.
- These keys are then used to direct data retrieval to a bucket where the data has been placed (elements in an array, typically).
- A common algorithm to hash string values is to add up all the ASCII values of each character and modulo divide this result by the size of the data set:

```
FOR i ← 0 TO LEN(stringToHash)-1
      hash = hash + CHAR_TO_CODE(stringToHash[i])
END FOR

hash = hash % tableSize
```

- Each new string is hashed into a key value to determine the appropriate index value to use to store in an array.
- Sometimes a hash value will be calculated to a value that already holds data, known as a **collision**.
- In cases where this happens, the table must be expanded to provide more hash values and all values must be rehashed.

Example: hashing process

Hash table to store string values.

New value 'sauce' needs to be stored in the hash table.

→ (83 + 65 + 85 + 67 + 69) % 6 = 3

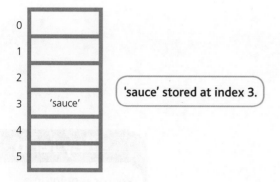

'sauce' stored at index 3.

New value 'cause' needs to be stored in the hash table.

→ (67 + 65 + 85 + 83 + 69) % 6 = 3

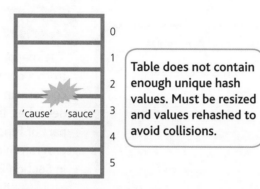

Table does not contain enough unique hash values. Must be resized and values rehashed to avoid collisions.

Dictionaries

Key points:

■ A dictionary is a data structure that records values alongside individual keys.

■ Each key is unique and is associated with an assigned value in the format {key:value}.

■ Dictionaries have the ability to quickly retrieve data associated with a key, for example the following shows how a list of network identifiers can be checked against plain text passwords.

```
users = {"id13243":"duck", "id13115":"goose", "id23342":"rat"}
userToAuth ← USERINPUT
userPassword ← USERINPUT
IF userPassword = users[userToAuth] THEN
      OUTPUT "Password verified"
ELSE
      OUTPUT "Password incorrect"
```

Vectors

Vectors can be represented as:

- a list of numbers
- functions that map domain values to co-domain values
- geometric points in space

Key points:

- Visually, a vector as a point in space is illustrated as a directed arrow.

Key term

Vector A point in a coordinate system describing an area in a space.

Synoptic link

The mapping of values from a domain to a co-domain, as a dictionary describes, is an integral part of functional programming as described in Section 2.8.

Example: vectors summarised as arrows

The two-vector [3.0, 5.0] over $\mathbb{R}$ ($\mathbb{R}^2$ where $\mathbb{R}$ is the set of real numbers) would be drawn as:

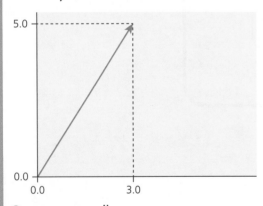

Or more generally:

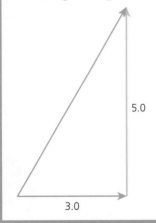

- Dictionaries are a useful means of representing a vector viewed as a function. For example, for the function $f : S \rightarrow \mathbb{R}$ where the set $S = \{0, 1\}$ the dictionary could be created as:

```
{0:3.0, 1:5.0}
```

- If vectors are to be represented as a list of numbers they can be stored simply in either a list or a 1D array. For example, in Python as a list, the same vector would be created as the array:

```
[3.0, 5.0]
```

- In Visual Basic, the same vector could be created in an array as:

```
Dim ballPos() as Double = New Double()(3.0, 5.0)
```

Synoptic link

Vectors are used to describe certain types of graphical images. See Section 2.1 to understand how.

Vector operations

Vectors can be operated on to determine new values.

Table 5 Vector operations

Operation	Description
Addition	Translates (moves) the original to a new position.
Scalar-vector multiplication	Scales the original vector by a given multiplier.
Convex combination of two vectors	Finds vectors that would fall within the vector space of two given vectors u and v where $\alpha u + \beta v$ and $\alpha + \beta = 1$.
Dot product of two vectors	Determines the relationship between two vectors when considered in a common direction and, by extension, the angle between them where $u \cdot v = u_1 v_1 + u_2 v_2 + \cdots + u_n v_n$.

Do you know?

1 Elements of an array data structure are accessed using which component?

2 What are the different types of files that computer programs can read from and write to?

3 Data structures can be either static or dynamic. What is the difference?

4 Queues can be implemented in three different ways. What are they?

5 What is a stack?

6 How could a graph data structure be implemented in a computer program?

Exam tip

Make sure you are aware of the uses of different data types within typical computer programs. You should be able to select the most appropriate data type for a given scenario.

1.3 Fundamentals of algorithms

You need to know

- Graphs are traversed breadth-first or depth-first.
- Trees are traversed in order, pre-order or post-order.
- Expressions can be expressed in Reverse Polish Notation or infix.
- Linear, binary or binary tree are data search algorithms.
- Bubble sort and merge sort are algorithms that organise data.
- Dijkstra's algorithm finds the shortest route through graphs.

Synoptic link

Graphs as abstract data types are described in more detail in Section 1.2.

Graph-traversal

There are two ways of traversing a graph to visit the nodes it links.

Breadth-first

1 Nodes that are connected to the starting point are visited first and stored in a queue in the order that they are visited.
2 Once all immediate nodes are visited, the first node in the queue is then checked in the same way until all its immediate nodes have been visited.
3 The algorithm completes once the queue is emptied.

Key term

Graph-traversal The process of visiting connected nodes within a graph, the order of which varies depending on the technique used.

Example: stages of breadth-first traversal

Step 1: Mark starting node S as visited.

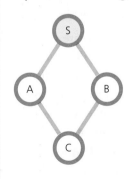

Step 2: Visit connected nodes and record in queue as they are visited.

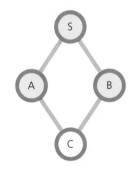

Step 3: Dequeue first node (A in this case) and visit all its unvisited neighbours.

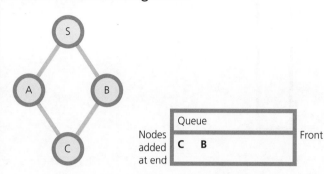

Step 4: Continue until queue is empty.

Queue

Breadth-first is useful in applications where your expected solution isn't far from the starting node or requires closer nodes to be visited first (finding the shortest path through a graph, for example).

Depth-first

1 Connected nodes are visited as far as possible until a dead end occurs.
2 A stack is used to record visited nodes and allows traversal to continue from the previous node once an end is found.
3 The algorithm completes once all nodes have been popped off the stack.

Depth-first is useful where the breadth of the graph is wide and the solution is unlikely to be near the starting node (e.g. determining a path through a maze).

Example: stages of depth-first traversal

Step 1: Mark starting node S as visited and add to stack.

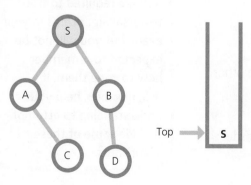

Step 2: Visit next adjacent node (A in this case) and mark as visited. Continue to next adjacent node (C), recording as visited.

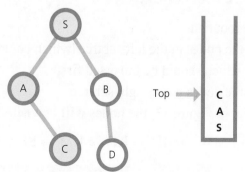

Step 3: Once dead end is reached, pop off elements of stack until node is found with unvisited neighbours (B has not been visited from S). Continue as before.

Step 4: Continue until stack is empty.

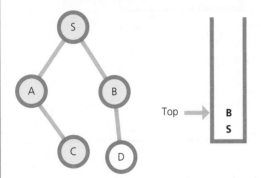

Top →

B
S

Tree-traversal

Traversing a tree ensures that all nodes are visited and processed in a suitable order depending on the results required.

The structure of a tree consists of a series of subtrees from any given node.

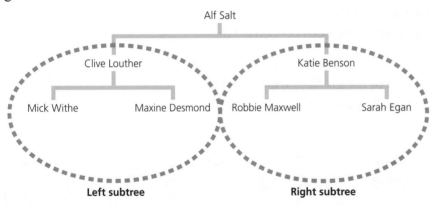

Alf Salt

Clive Louther

Katie Benson

Mick Withe   Maxine Desmond   Robbie Maxwell   Sarah Egan

Left subtree   **Right subtree**

Figure 13 **Tree structure organising managers within a company**

Pre-order traversal

1 Visit the root node.
2 Visit all the nodes in the left subtree (which could include other subtrees which should be traversed first).
3 Visit all the nodes in the right subtree.

For example, in Figure 13, the nodes will be visited in the order:

$AS \rightarrow CL \rightarrow MW \rightarrow MD \rightarrow KB \rightarrow RM \rightarrow SE$

Pre-order traversal is useful when parent nodes and their children need to be kept together and visited in order, for example when copying a tree.

In-order traversal

1   Visit all the nodes in the left subtree (starting with any other subtrees within that).
2   Visit the root node.
3   Visit all the nodes in the right subtree.

For example in Figure 13, the nodes will be visited in the order:

$$MW \rightarrow CL \rightarrow MD \rightarrow AS \rightarrow RM \rightarrow KB \rightarrow SE$$

In-order traversal is useful when ordering data, for example outputting the contents of a binary tree of numbers in numerical order.

Post-order traversal

1   Visit all the nodes in the left subtree (starting with any other subtrees within that).
2   Visit all the nodes in the right subtree.
3   Visit the root node.

For example, in Figure 13, the nodes will be visited in the order:

$$MW \rightarrow MD \rightarrow CL \rightarrow RM \rightarrow SE \rightarrow KB \rightarrow AS$$

Post-order traversal is useful when removing nodes, leaving the roots intact.

Reverse Polish Notation

Key points:

■ Expressions written as infix form combine operands (values) using a single operator in between, for example 2 + 3.
■ Reverse Polish Notation (RPN), also known as postfix form, is where operands are listed first followed by an operator, for example 2 3 +.
■ RPN eliminates the need for brackets and can be easily evaluated when the values are stored on a stack.

Example: RPN expression stored in a stack

Consider the expression 2 * (3 + 6)

The RPN form of this would be 2 3 6 + *

Evaluated when stored on a stack:

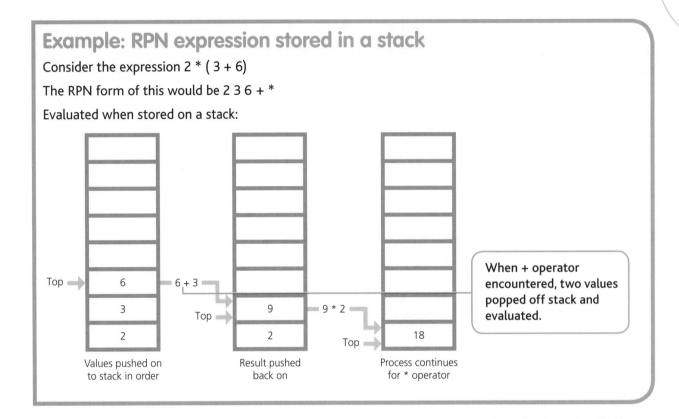

Top → | 6 | 6 + 3
| 3 | Top →
| 2 |

| 9 | 9 * 2
| 2 | Top →

| 18 |

When + operator encountered, two values popped off stack and evaluated.

Values pushed on to stack in order

Result pushed back on

Process continues for * operator

Search algorithms

Search algorithms perform differently depending on the size of the data set and the way it is organised.

Big-O notation is used to express how the time complexity of an algorithm grows as a function of the size of the data set being processed (n).

Linear search

Operation of linear search

Given a sequence of random data, linear search works through the sequence from start to finish, stopping once it finds the data it is looking for.

```
numberToFind ← USERINPUT

i ← 0

dataFound ← False

WHILE (i < LEN(dataSeq)) AND (dataFound = False)
    IF dataSeq[i] = numberToFind THEN
        dataFound ← True
    ELSE
        i ← i + 1
    ENDIF
```

```
ENDWHILE
IF dataFound = True THEN
     OUTPUT "Data found in position: " + i
ELSE
     OUTPUT "Data not found"
ENDIF
```

Performance of linear search

■ The average number of comparisons of an array of length n is the total number of possible comparisons for all points in the array divided by the number of elements.

■ The total number of comparisons $1 + 2 + 3 + \ldots + n = \dfrac{n(n + 1)}{2}$ and the average number of comparisons is $\dfrac{(n + 1)}{2}$.

■ Using Big-O notation, constants are ignored, so linear search has an average time complexity of O(n).

Binary search

Operation of binary search

■ Given a sequence of ordered data, binary search begins with the middle value.

■ Should the value being searched for be less than this, the set of data above the midpoint is discarded; similarly, the lower half would be discarded if the value is determined to be above the midpoint.

■ A new midpoint is selected in the smaller set of data and the process continues until the data is found.

```
numberToFind ← USERINPUT

first ← 0

last ← len(dataSeq)-1

dataFound ← False

WHILE (first <= last) AND (dataFound = False)
    midpoint ← (first + last)//2
    IF dataSeq[midpoint] = item THEN
         dataFound ← True
    ELSE
         IF item < dataSeq[midpoint] THEN
```

```
                last ← midpoint - 1
        ELSE
                first ← midpoint + 1
        ENDIF
    ENDIF
ENDWHILE
IF dataFound = True THEN
    OUTPUT "Data found in position: " + midpoint
ELSE
    OUTPUT "Data not found"
ENDIF
```

Performance of binary search

- In the worst case, the remaining number of comparisons of an array of length n would halve each time until one element remained.
- For an array of size $s = 2^n$ where n is the number of comparisons, it would take $\log_2(s)$ comparisons.
- The time complexity of binary search is therefore $O(\log n)$.

Binary tree search

Key points:
- Performed on a particular type of binary tree: the binary search tree (BST).
- The order of the nodes for a BST is important so that it can be searched in order.

A BST must:
- place child nodes precede a parent to the connected left subtree
- place child nodes succeed a parent to the connected right subtree
- not include duplicate values

A binary search tree is constructed with each child node being ordered depending on the value in each parent node.

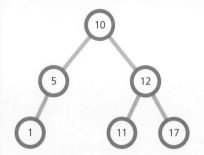

Example: binary search tree construction

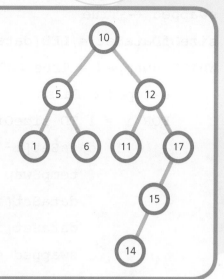

As values are added, they are placed to the next available left position if smaller than a parent value or to the right if larger.

In this example the numbers 6, 15, 14 have been added in this way.

Searching in a BST is therefore relatively simple and is performed with O(log n) time complexity.

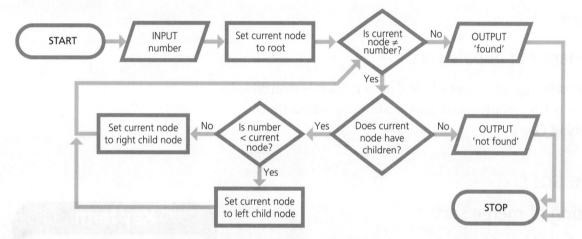

Figure 14 Flowchart of algorithm to search a BST

Sorting algorithms

Sorting algorithms organise data into order.

The time complexity of different algorithms changes depending on the original organisation of the data and the size of the data set.

Bubble sort

Operation of bubble sort

- Works through the data set comparing adjacent values and swapping when out of order.
- Completes once data has been passed through and no swaps have been made.
- Bubble sort can be made more efficient by not comparing previously sorted elements at the end of the data set.

```
swapped ← True
sizeOfDataSet = LEN(dataSet)
WHILE swapped = True AND sizeOfDataSet > 1
      swapped ← False
      FOR i = 1 TO sizeOfDataSet-1
          IF dataSet[i-1] > dataSet[i]
              tempSwap ← dataSet[i]
              dataSet[i] ← dataSet[i-1]
              dataSet[i] ← tempSwap
              swapped ← True
          ENDIF
      ENDFOR
      sizeOfDataSet ← sizeOfDataSet -1
ENDWHILE
```

Performance of bubble sort

Under typical usage situations where data is randomly distributed, bubble sort is particularly inefficient, performing with a time complexity of $O(n^2)$.

Merge sort

Operation of merge sort

Merge and sort is a **divide and conquer algorithm**.

- The original problem is reduced to smaller, more-solvable problems and joined back together to form the solution.
- The set of data is divided in half and then each of these halves are divided again.
- The process continues until the data has been separated into individual components.
- Each of these components are then re-joined in order until the data has been sorted.

> **Key term**
>
> **Divide and conquer algorithm** The original problem is divided into smaller problems that can be solved more easily. The final solution is the combination of these smaller solutions.

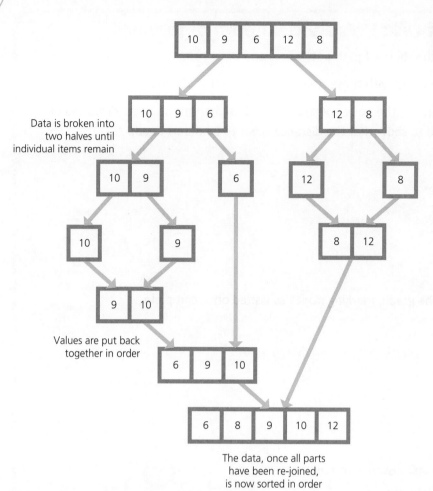

Data is broken into two halves until individual items remain

Values are put back together in order

The data, once all parts have been re-joined, is now sorted in order

Figure 15 Merge sort process

Performance of merge sort

The recursive nature of this algorithm results in a time complexity of $O(n \log n)$.

Optimisation algorithms

Optimisation algorithms are those that select the best outcome with regard to a specific criterion.

Dijkstra's shortest path algorithm

Finds the shortest path between nodes within a weighted graph by:
- visiting all nodes in the graph and updating the shortest distance of the path that arrives at that node
- the shortest path is determined by working backwards from the end node using the shortest distances for all other nodes

Example: operation of Dijkstra's shortest path algorithm

The algorithm is required to find the shortest path between A and D.

Step 1: Visit each node in order, starting with those that have the shortest distance.

Step 2: Update the shortest distance to the node you are visiting based on the shortest distances of reaching previous nodes (∞ is used to show that the distance is yet to be determined).

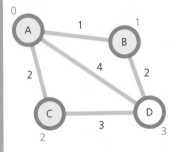

Step 3: Continue for all nodes in the graph, marking nodes as visited once complete.

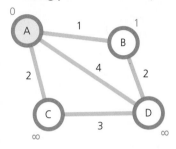

Step 4: Work backwards from the last distance to find the path that determined this same distance.

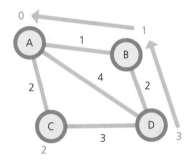

Applications of this algorithm include scenarios where the most efficient path through a graph-like structure must be found, for example, the shortest path between nodes in a network or the shortest road route between two points on a map.

Do you know?

1 What is the difference between 'breadth-first' and 'depth-first' graph-traversal?

2 What are the three possible types of tree-traversal?

3 How is the infix expression 7 + 8 / (9 − 2) expressed in Reverse Polish Notation?

4 If binary search is more efficient than linear search, why is linear search sometimes used?

5 In order to find data in a binary search tree, how must the tree be constructed?

6 With reference to time complexity, which of bubble sort or merge sort completes more quickly as the size of the data to be sorted grows?

1.4 Theory of computation

You need to know
- Abstraction hides details of problems if they aren't immediately useful to the solution.
- Decomposition breaks down problems.
- Finite state machines accept regular languages.
- Regular expressions represent regular languages.
- Backus–Naur form represents context-free languages.
- Algorithms are compared by their complexity relative to the size of a problem they solve.
- Turing machines provide a definition of what is computable.

Abstraction and automation

Computation is the processing of data to solve a given problem.

Arriving at a solution requires thought about what the problem entails, focusing on the most significant parts first.

Problem solving

Developing a solution to a logic problem requires several steps:

1 describing the problem
2 planning a solution
3 implementing the solution
4 evaluating the solution's effectiveness

It is important that the quality of the solution is checked both in terms of the outcomes it provides and how efficiently it reaches the solution.

Synoptic link

The development of software and the stages that are carried out are described in more detail in Section 2.9.

Abstraction

Key points:
- Representational abstraction is the process of ignoring details that are not necessarily important for the solution.
- Abstraction by generalisation allows the problem solver to spot similarities with other problems to help employ a similar solution.

Key term

Abstraction Hiding the details of a problem that are not immediately important in helping to arrive at a solution.

Table 6 Abstraction techniques

Technique	Description
Information hiding	Objects within the scope of the problem are defined just by the characteristics that are necessary (the inner workings of each object do not need to be known).
Procedural abstraction	Considering the main elements of what a solution to a problem should do without considering the values used.
Functional abstraction	Considers that values will be changed and focuses on recognising the way they do rather than how they are changed.
Data abstraction	Ignoring the details of how data is constructed enables new, more useful kinds of data objects to be designed.

Problem abstraction/reduction

The ability to create an abstracted model of a problem focuses the solution only on what is important.

Example: abstracting a number problem

Adding all the even numbers up to a given specified value requires the problem to be simplified.

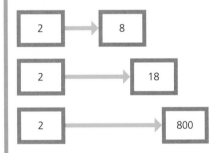

A smaller problem can be explored first so a generalised solution can be found and applied to problems of any size.

0	1	2	3	4	5	6	7	8	9

Adding the even numbers below 10 doesn't require consideration of the odd numbers in between and can therefore be ignored.

0 can also be ignored as it doesn't add anything to the sum.

2	4	6	8

The difference between each even number is 2.

If the solution keeps adding 2, the even numbers will be generated.

This will work up to any number which we can specify with an arbitrary identifier.

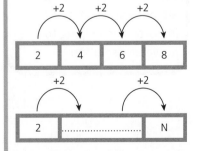

Decomposition/composition

Key points:

- A problem expressed at the required level of detail can be analysed as a series of smaller sub-problems in a process known as **decomposition**.
- Once these smaller problems are solved, they can be combined together again to form a completed model of the solution.

Example: decomposing a problem

The problem of adding even numbers from 2 up to a certain value is decomposed into the following stages:

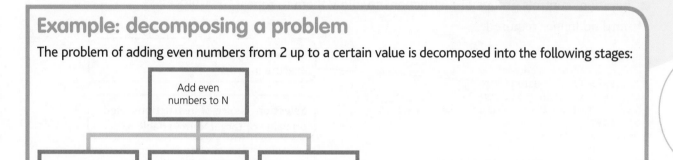

Automation

Automation requires implementing abstracted models so that solutions can be arrived at.

Automation is achieved by:

- creating **algorithms** that detail the steps to follow to produce an expected solution
- implementing these algorithms in program code (instructions that a computer can follow)
- implementing the models of any data structures that describe the relationships between data
- executing the code to allow the computer to produce the required solution.

Following and writing algorithms

Algorithms provide steps to follow to complete a task.

Exam tip

Algorithms form the basis of a large part of computer science. It is not enough just to appreciate what they are. You should recognise how they are designed and implemented. Ensure that you have plenty of experience designing and coding algorithms yourself.

Solutions to problems can be expressed using pseudocode with the following standard constructs.

- Sequence: an instruction completes in turn after the previous instruction has completed.
- Assignment: sets (or changes) a value stored in a memory location identified by a variable name.
- Selection: enables a decision to control the subsequent instruction(s) to execute upon evaluation.
- Iteration: controls groups of instructions to allow them to repeat until no longer required.

Synoptic link

Section 1.1 provides further insight into how the fundamental components of programming are used to realise algorithmic processes.

```
01. targetNum ← USERINPUT
02. IF targetNum < 2 THEN
03.     OUTPUT "Even positive numbers only"
04. ELSE
05.     evenNum = 0
06.     total = 0
07.     WHILE evenNum < targetNum
08.         evenNum ← evenNum + 2
09.         total = total + evenNum
10.     ENDWHILE
11. ENDIF
12. OUTPUT "Total is:" + total
```

Sequence: by default instructions execute in order.

Selection: choice of instruction based on value of targetNum variable.

Assignment: value 0 is assigned to memory location identified by variable name evenNum.

Iteration: block repeats until target number is reached.

Figure 16 **Pseudocode algorithm to solve the even number problem**

Algorithms can be hand-traced using a **trace table** to explore the values assigned to variables throughout the running of the program and any output.

Key terms

Trace table A technique used to test algorithms/code to ensure the output is as expected for given conditions.

Pseudocode A method used to design code using informally written instructions.

Table 7 **A trace table**

targetNum	evenNum	Total	Output
6	0	0	
	2	2	
	4	6	
	6	12	12

Key points:
- To be used by a computer, the algorithm must be converted to instructions that the computer can follow.
- Programming languages are used to implement the algorithm designed in **pseudocode**.
- The algorithm, once coded, should be tested for accuracy of output and, for any given input, it must produce the expected output.
- The performance of an implemented algorithm can be tested using a series of test data to ensure it works under all conditions.
- The efficiency of the algorithm should also be considered.

For example, the program as designed previously yields the correct result but is not the most efficient method as the correct output can be determined mathematically:

$$\left(\frac{\text{targetValue}}{2}\right)^2 + \left(\frac{\text{targetValue}}{2}\right)$$

The performance of such a calculation reduces the time complexity of the algorithm significantly when targetValue gets larger due to the removal of an iteration structure.

Regular languages

Finite state machines (FSMs)

Key points:
- Provide an abstracted model of a system outlining the states it can take and how it transitions between them.
- The operation of the system can be summarised using a state transition diagram together with a state transition table.

Example: accessing a network computer with a username and password

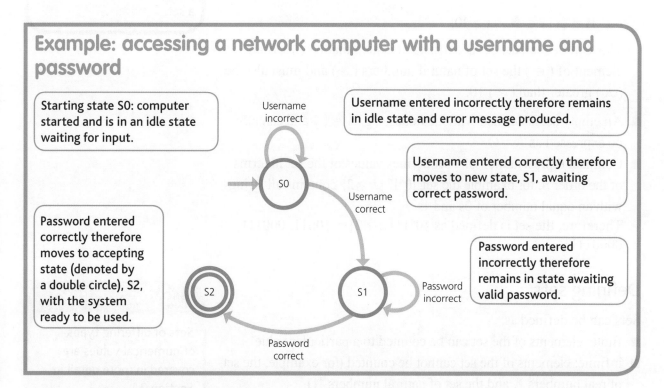

Starting state S0: computer started and is in an idle state waiting for input.

Username entered incorrectly therefore remains in idle state and error message produced.

Username entered correctly therefore moves to new state, S1, awaiting correct password.

Password entered correctly therefore moves to accepting state (denoted by a double circle), S2, with the system ready to be used.

Password entered incorrectly therefore remains in state awaiting valid password.

Table 8 State transition table

Input	Current state	Next state	Output
Incorrect username	S0	S0	Error message
Correct username	S0	S1	null
Incorrect password	S1	S1	Error message
Correct password	S1	S2	null

FSMs can produce output upon a change of state. For example, incorrectly entering a username might produce an error message. The state transition arrow would indicate this.

Regular language

Key points:
- A regular language is defined as a formal language that can be expressed by regular expressions.
- A regular expression is a sequence of characters that describes how a set of data should be searched.
- A regular language could also be a language that an FSM will accept, therefore, a regular expression can be represented by an FSM.

Maths for regular expressions

Key points:
- Regular expressions work on **sets** of data.
- A set is defined by a name and the values it contains, occurring no more than once and unordered, e.g. A = {1, 2, 3, 4, 5}.
- Set comprehensions can also define a set without having to write the individual values.
  For example, the set comprehension for all the natural numbers that are greater than 10 would be:

  $$B = \{x \mid x \in \mathbb{N} \wedge x > 10\}$$

  This can be read as: set B consists of x such that ($x \mid$) x is an element of ($\in$) the set of natural numbers ($\mathbb{N}$) and must also be ($\wedge$) greater than ($>$) 10.

- An empty set is defined without values, e.g. A = { } and can also be expressed as A = Ø.
- Compact representation of a set defines values of the set in terms of the order n, for example the set $\{0^n 1^n \mid n \geq 2\}$ contains all strings with an equal number of 0s and 1s.
  Therefore, the set is defined as $\{0^n 1^n \mid n \geq 2\} = \{0011, 000111, 00001111, \ldots\}$.

> ## Key terms
>
> **Set** A mathematical object that describes a collection of other separate objects.
>
> **Cardinality** A measure of how many numbers are in a set.

Defining sets

Sets can be defined as:
- finite: elements of the set can be counted to a particular value
- infinite: elements of the set cannot be counted (for example, the set of real numbers $\mathbb{R}$ and the set of natural numbers $\mathbb{N}$)
- countably infinite: one that can be counted using natural numbers (for example, the set of natural numbers $\mathbb{N}$).

The **cardinality** of a finite set is a measure of the number of elements that a set contains.

The Cartesian product of two sets is the set of all the order pairs (a, b) where a is a member of A and b is a member of B.

> ## Synoptic link
>
> Sets of differing types of numerical values are covered in more detail in Section 2.1.

Subsets

Key points:

- Subsets are sets that are contained within a wider set of values.
- It can be said that $\{2, 3, 4\} \subset \mathbb{N}$ where $\subset$ means 'is the proper subset of the set of natural numbers $\mathbb{N}$'.
- A proper subset will not contain all the values of the **superset** it draws from.
- Where the subset is not proper, it may be the equivalent full set it is related to, for example $\{2, 3, 4\} \subseteq \{2, 3, 4\}$ where $\subseteq$ includes both $\subset$ and $=$.
- A countable set is a set with the same cardinality as some subset of natural numbers.

Set operations

New sets can be constructed from operations performed on two sets.

The shaded area represents a value that is a member of a specified set.

Figure 17 shows a single element, written as $x \in A$.

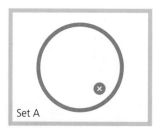

Figure 17

The area in Figure 18 represents the union of the two sets (the sets joined together), written as $A \cup B$.

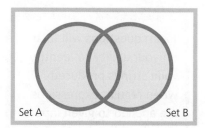

Figure 18

The area in Figure 19 represents the intersection of the two sets (the values that are common to both sets), written as $A \cap B$.

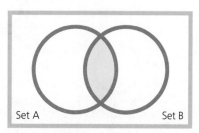

Figure 19

The area in Figure 20 represents the difference between A and B (the values in A that are not in B), written as $A \setminus B$. This can also be written as $\{x \mid x \in A \land x \notin B\}$.

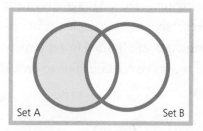

Figure 20

Regular expressions

Regular expressions are, fundamentally, ways of describing a set of data.

When applying a regular expression to a string, it will match and summarise a subset of the data it is applied to.

Regular expressions use combinations of metacharacters to produce matches including:

- * (0 or more repetitions)
- \+ (1 or more repetitions)
- ? (0 or 1 repetitions, making the character optional)
- | (alternation, allowing a choice between characters)
- ( ) (to group expressions).

For every regular expression there is an equivalent FSM.

Example: regular expression and finite state machine equivalence

Consider a regular expression ab|cb+ used to match appropriate strings. The equivalent FSM would look like this.

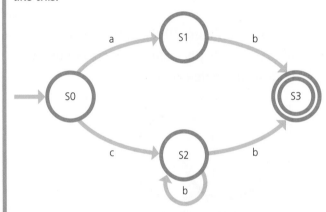

Both representations would generate the set of valid strings {ab, cb, cbb, cbbb, ...}.

Context-free languages

Key points:
- Where language cannot be represented by using regular expressions, a context-free language may have the grammar necessary to represent more complex relationships.
- As regular languages are limited to set structures, context-free languages use recursive relationships to provide less limited representations.

Backus–Naur form (BNF)

Key points:
- A notation used to describe context-free grammars.
- BNF describes the elements of a language, for example:
  <digit>   ::= 0 | 1 | 2 | 3 | 4 | 5 | 6 | 7 | 8 | 9

Exam tip

Exam questions will focus on your ability to identify valid strings produced when regular expressions are applied to given inputs. You should understand how metacharacters are used to match input strings.

- The term 'digit' can be represented by one of the integers 0–9.
- Further terms can build on previous established terms, for example a phone number would need to make use of repetitions of digit terms:

  <phone>   ::= <digit> | <digit> <phone>

  Therefore, a 'phone' term will be a digit recursively described as a further phone term until the last digit is reached.

Example: using BNF to describe the language of a phone number

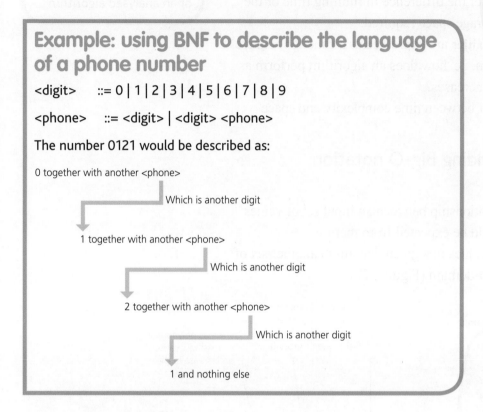

<digit>   ::= 0 | 1 | 2 | 3 | 4 | 5 | 6 | 7 | 8 | 9

<phone>   ::= <digit> | <digit> <phone>

The number 0121 would be described as:

0 together with another <phone>

Which is another digit

1 together with another <phone>

Which is another digit

2 together with another <phone>

Which is another digit

1 and nothing else

Syntax diagrams

As an alternative to BNF, a context-free language could be represented as a syntax diagram with the same rules applied.

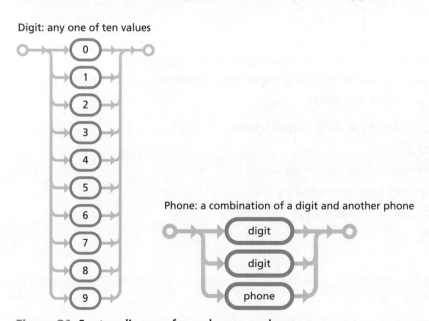

Digit: any one of ten values

Phone: a combination of a digit and another phone

Figure 21 Syntax diagram for a phone number

Classification of algorithms

Comparing algorithms

Key points:

- The comparison of performance between different algorithms can be expressed by either the difference in running time or the amount of additional storage space required.
- These **algorithm complexities** are expressed as a function relative to the size of the problem, i.e. how does an algorithm perform as the work it needs to do increases?
- There is often a trade-off between time complexity and space complexity.

> **Key term**
>
> Algorithm complexity An estimation of the resources required for the completion of an analysed algorithm.

Maths for understanding Big-O notation

Key points:

- Functions define the relationship between an input set of values and the results that should be expected from them.
- This relationship maps values in a given domain to another set of value drawn from the co-domain (Figure 22).

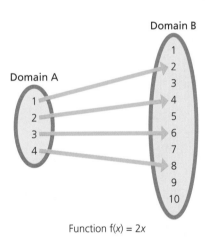

Function f(x) = 2x

Figure 22 A function mapping from a domain to another set of values in the co-domain

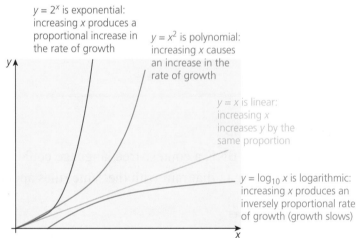

Figure 23 Comparison of linear, polynomial, exponential and logarithmic functions as their input x increases

- Functions can be described by the reaction of their output when the domain input changes (Figure 23).
- A permutation of a set is one order the values can be arranged in.
- All possible permutations of a set can be determined by the factorial of the number of values, e.g. for three values there are 3! permutations or $3 \times 2 \times 1 = 6$.

Deriving time complexity

Key points:

- Code must be evaluated to determine how changes to the size of the input affects the amount of time instructions need to be run.

- An algorithm with O(1) (constant) time complexity doesn't change its run time no matter how much input data is being processed.
- It doesn't matter how big `dataArray` gets, outputting one element takes the same amount of time.

```
dataArray = [1,2,3...]

element ← USERINPUT

OUTPUT dataArray[element]
```

- If each instruction takes a count of 1 to complete, the algorithm will always take a count of 3 which is a constant amount of time.
- An algorithm with O(n) (linear) time complexity increases its runtime in equal proportion every time the size of the input data increases.

```
dataArray = [1,2,3...]

element ← USERINPUT

FOR i ← 0 TO LEN(dataArray)−1

    OUTPUT dataArray[element]

END FOR
```

In this case, as dataArray gets bigger, the FOR loop will need to run more times.

If `dataArray` has three elements it will run three times and, similarly, if it has 100 elements it will run 100 times.

- Typically, algorithms with nested iterative statements (loops inside loops) will have polynomial, O(n^2), time complexity.
- Recursive algorithms will have exponential, O(2^n), time complexity.
- Algorithms that work with partitions of half the data set (such as binary search) tend to have O(log n) time complexity.

Categorising algorithms

The complexity of algorithms, and the hardware that exists to run them, limit what solutions can be practically implemented.

Algorithms can be classified as either:
- tractable: problems that have a polynomial (or less) time complexity
- intractable: problems where the time complexity is more than polynomial.

Intractable problems have no efficient algorithms to solve them (though there may be inefficient algorithms).

There also exist problems that cannot be solved algorithmically such as the **Halting problem**.

Synoptic link

Comparison of the complexity of algorithms is a key part of the fundamental common algorithms seen in Section 1.3. Be aware of the differences in performance of algorithms under different conditions.

Key term

Halting problem Given a program and some input, does an algorithm exist to prove that the program will continue indefinitely or finish running?

Halting problem

Key points:
- The Halting problem is an unsolvable problem of determining if a program will eventually stop given an input.
- This can be demonstrated using a program that loops based on a condition that never evaluates as False.

```
x ← 1
WHILE x > 0
    inLoop ← True
ENDWHILE
```

It cannot be proved that this program will loop forever as the only way to determine this is to allow the loop to run forever.
- This problem allows programmers to recognise that there are some problems that cannot be solved by computers.

Models of computation

Turing machine

Key points:
- A hypothetical machine that can simulate any computer algorithm, providing a definition of what is computable.

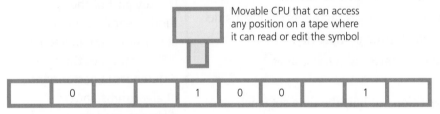

Movable CPU that can access any position on a tape where it can read or edit the symbol

Infinitely long tape that acts as data storage within a computer where the symbols 0, 1 and " " can be written

Figure 24 Structure of a Turing machine

- A Turing machine is essentially a computer with a single fixed program which can be summarised by a state transition diagram.

States of a Turing machine

Consider the Turing machine that needs to invert a sequence of bits.

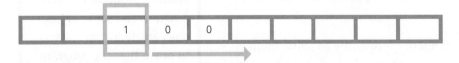

The machine starts at the first bit and continues right, changing each bit, until a blank square is reached signifying the end.

Summarised as a state transition diagram:

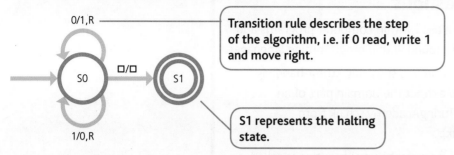

Transition rule describes the step of the algorithm, i.e. if 0 read, write 1 and move right.

S1 represents the halting state.

A transition function describes how the transition rules change the state of the Turing machine under all circumstances:

$$\delta(S0, 0) = (S0, 1, \rightarrow)$$
$$\delta(S0, 1) = (S0, 0, \rightarrow)$$
$$\delta(S0, \square) = (S1, \square)$$

Current state / Input / Next state / Output

■ As Turing machines are fixed to solve a single problem, a universal Turing machine is a general machine that can simulate any possible Turing machine.

Do you know?

1 What is the purpose of abstraction when solving a problem?

2 Decomposition breaks a problem down into several smaller sub-problems. In order to arrive at a final solution, what must happen to these parts?

3 What does a finite state machine model?

4 Identify the three shortest strings that would be matched with the regular expression a(a|b)*.

5 Order the following functions in terms of their time complexity starting with the one that has the slowest rate of growth: $O(\log n)$, $O(2^n)$, $O(n)$, $O(n^2)$, $O(1)$.

6 What are the main characteristics of a Turing machine?

End of section 1 questions

1 Describe how data types are used within computer programs and give three examples of those found within programming languages.

2 Explain how the length, position and substring string-handling operations could be used to extract the domain part of an email address (e.g. extract TuringAcademy.sch.uk from alan@TuringAcademy.sch.uk).

3 Describe how a stack frame is used when a subroutine is called by a program. You should also describe what happens once the subroutine completes.

4 Describe the four operations that can be performed on a queue data structure.

5 Identify two ways that a graph can be represented within a computer program.

6 Calculate the dot product of the vectors [3, 4, 5] and [5, 6, 7].

7 Describe the differences between depth-first and breadth-first graph-traversal algorithms.

8 Explain the differences between linear search and binary search in terms of their time complexity and how it changes as the size of the input increases.

9 Give one example of the use of each of the following tree-traversal algorithms: pre-order, post-order, in order.

10 Identify three possible methods of abstraction that can be employed to hide the unimportant details of a problem.

11 Draw the finite state machine (FSM) that represents the regular expression a?b+c*.

12 Identify and describe the two ways in which algorithmic problems can be classified.

2 Computer science principles

2.1 Fundamentals of data representation

> ### You need to know
>
> - Data in a computer is based on the binary number system.
> - Binary has the same fundamental properties as any other number system.
> - Bits are the fundamental units of binary information.
> - Bits are grouped into bytes and then summarised using prefixes.
> - Binary can be used to represent signed, unsigned and fractional numbers.
> - Binary can be used as a coding scheme to represent different types of non-numeric data.

Number systems

Key points:

- A definition of a number system describes the range and type of expected values.
- Different types of numbers have different properties.
- Numbers used for counting are whole values.
- Numbers used for measurement require fractional parts.

Natural numbers

Key points:

- Natural numbers provide the most fundamental type of counting.
- Counting objects uses combinations of the symbols 0 to 9, for example: 6, 14, 185, …
- Natural numbers are described as the set: $\mathbb{N} = \{0, 1, 2, 3, … \}$.

> ### Synoptic link
>
> Descriptions of sets and their applications in computer science are discussed in more detail in Section 1.4.

Integer numbers

Key points:

- Natural numbers can be extended to include negative values.
- Integer numbers include all the natural numbers but also whole negative numbers.
- Integers are described by the set: $\mathbb{Z} = \{…, –2, –1, 0, 1, …\}$.

Rational numbers

Key points:

- Rational numbers are values that can describe any fraction (ratio of integers) such as $\frac{1}{2}$ and $\frac{8}{3}$.
- These include all natural and integer values as they too can be expressed as fractions, for example 5 can be expressed as $\frac{5}{1}$.
- Rational numbers are described by the set:
  $\mathbb{Q} = \{\ldots, 1/1, 1/2, 1/3, 1/4, \ldots\}$.

Irrational numbers

Key points:

- Irrational numbers are not rational numbers and cannot be written as a fraction.
- Irrational numbers therefore cannot be written as a limited decimal value.
- Examples are usually well-known values that are often given unique descriptors such as $\sqrt{2}$, π, e.

Real numbers

Key points:

- Any number that is considered either rational or irrational can be described as real.
- The whole set of real numbers is identified as $\mathbb{R}$.
- This definition, considered alongside $\mathbb{Q}$, allows irrational numbers to be defined as $\mathbb{R} \setminus \mathbb{Q}$ (all of $\mathbb{R}$ excluding $\mathbb{Q}$).

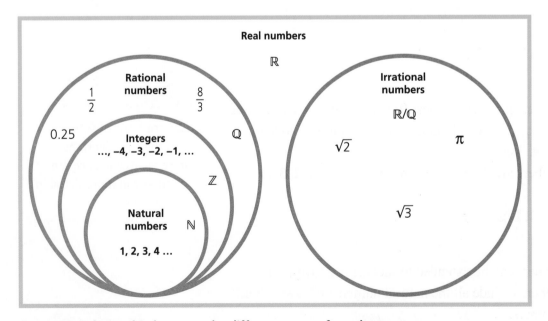

Figure 25 Relationship between the different types of numbers

Ordinal numbers

Key points:

- Where the position of a number needs to be described, ordinal values are used.
- In a well-ordered set S = {'a', 'b', 'c', 'd'} then 'a' is the 1st object and 'd' the 4th.
- Therefore, the ordinal numbers are 1st, 2nd, 3rd etc.

Number bases

Key points:

- Number bases refer to the number of unique symbols used to represent values in that base.
- The most familiar base used is **decimal** (base 10) which uses the symbols 0, 1, 2, 3, 4, 5, 6, 7, 8, 9.
- The **binary** number system (base 2) uses only the symbols 0 and 1.
- **Hexadecimal** numbering (base 16) extends the decimal system to include letter symbols, i.e. 0, 1, 2, 3, 4, 5, 6, 7, 8, 9, A, B, C, D, E, F.
- Numbers in any system should be described in the form $Number_{base}$.
  For example, the number 74 can be represented in different bases as follows:
  - [ ] base 10: $Number_{10}$, i.e. 74_{10}
  - [ ] base 2: $Number_2$, i.e. 1001010_2
  - [ ] base 16: $Number_{16}$, i.e. $4A_{16}$

> ## Exam tip
>
> Recognise that the sets described here are all related in some way. A description of one particular set may need to make reference to others. Make sure that you understand all of the descriptions here.

> ## Key terms
>
> **Decimal** Number values that use base 10.
>
> **Binary** Number values that use base 2.
>
> **Hexadecimal** Number values that use base 16.

Converting between bases

Key points:

- All bases describe the same numerical values, just in different ways.
- The position of a value affects the amount that it represents by a power of the base, where the right-most value is the base to the power of 0.
  For example, for the number 924_{10} the 9 (in position 3) represents 9×10^2 or 900 whereas in binary, for the number 10000_2 the 1 (in position 5) represents 1×2^4 or 16.

Converting from decimal

When converting from decimal to binary, the decimal value should be split into a combination of binary place values.

Example: converting to binary

Convert 200_{10} to binary:

base^{position}	2^7	2^6	2^5	2^4	2^3	2^2	2^1	2^0
Value of position	128	64	32	16	8	4	2	1
Number required	1	1	0	0	1	0	0	0
Amount contributed	128	64	0	0	8	0	0	0

Step 1: If value can be used in the decimal, then binary value is 1 to show it is used. 0 is recorded if place value doesn't contribute.

Step 2: If value is used, remove it from overall decimal value. In this example remaining places need to contribute $200 - 128 = 72$

Step 3: Continue process for all values until all bits considered.

Binary value is 11001000_2.

The same process applies when converting to hexadecimal, the only difference being each place value can contribute up to 15 of that value.

Example: converting to hexadecimal

Convert 200_{10} to hexadecimal:

base^{position}	16^1	16^0
Value of position	16	1
Number required	12 (C)	8 (8)
Amount contributed	192	8

Step 1: Consider if $1 \times$ position value to $15 \times$ the position value can be used to make the original decimal value. If so, use that multiple in this position.

Step 2: If value used, remove this from overall decimal value. In this example remaining places need to contribute $200 - 192 = 8$

Step 3: Continue process for all values until all places considered.

In this example, $12 \times 16 = 192$ which can be used to make 200.

Hexadecimal value is $C8_{16}$.

Converting from binary

To convert binary to decimal, the place values are added where the bit is 1. For the previous example, this is $128 + 64 + 8$ giving 200.

When converting to hexadecimal, groups of 4 bits can be directly converted to single hexadecimal values.

Example: converting to hexadecimal

Convert $1\,0\,1\,1\,0\,1\,1\,0_2$ to hexadecimal:

Step 1: Group the bits into collections of 4 bits, starting from the right.

$1\,0\,1\,1 \qquad 0\,1\,1\,0$

Step 2: Convert each value directly to the hexadecimal equivalent.

$0\,1\,1\,0$ becomes 6_{16}

$1\,0\,1\,1$ becomes B_{16}

Step 3: Join these groups to form the equivalent hexadecimal value.

In this example, $1\,0\,1\,1\,0\,1\,1\,0_2$ becomes $B6_{16}$.

Conversion is straightforward between these bases as base 16 is a multiple of base 2.

Hexadecimal can be considered a shorthand for binary due to the direct representation of groupings of bits.

Converting from hexadecimal

To convert to binary from hexadecimal, the opposite of binary to hexadecimal conversion using groups of 4 bits is performed.

When converting to decimal from hexadecimal, multiples of the place value are used. For the previous example, this is $(12 \times 16) + (8 \times 1) = 200$.

Units of information

Key points:

- Bits are used as the most fundamental unit of information within computer systems.
- For n bits there can be 2^n different values, for example for two bits there are $2^2 (= 4)$ different values (00, 01, 10, 11).
- Computers work with groups of 8 bits, referred to as bytes.

Multiples of bytes

Quantities of bytes can be described using prefixes to represent common multiples. These prefixes can be used in binary where they represent powers of 2, or in decimal, where powers of 10 are used.

Table 9 Some common binary prefixes

kibi	Ki	2^{10}
mebi	Mi	2^{20}
gibi	Gi	2^{30}
tebi	Ti	2^{40}

Table 10 Some common decimal prefixes

kilo	k	10^3
mega	M	10^6
giga	G	10^9
tera	T	10^{12}

The same value represented using these different bases of prefixes will be different, for example 2500 bytes could be summarised as 2.44 KiB or 2.5 kB.

Binary number system

In order to represent a range of useful values, binary is extended to cover negative and fractional values.

Unsigned binary

Key points:

- Values that are zero or greater can be represented using combinations of bits in an unsigned binary form.
- Should values less than zero (i.e. negative values) need to be represented, then some form of signed binary must be used to indicate if a number is positive or negative.
- For any n unsigned binary bits, the range of values representable are 0 to $2^n - 1$.

Unsigned binary arithmetic

Unsigned binary numbers are added in columns:

Example: adding unsigned binary numbers

```
     0   1   1   0   0   0   1   0
 +   0   1   1   0   1   0   0   1
   ─────────────────────────────────
     1   1   0   0   1   0   1   1
   1     1
```

Addition can involve the two values in the same place and any carry values. In this case: $1 + 1 + 1 = 11$.

Where the addition creates an answer with two bits, the most significant bit is carried into the next column.

Starting on the right, each of the two bits in the same place value are added.

$0 + 0 = 0$

$0 + 1 = 1$

$1 + 0 = 1$

$1 + 1 = 10$

Binary multiplication of unsigned values is carried out by multiplying the base value by the multiplier at each place value position and adding the results together.

Example: multiplying unsigned binary numbers

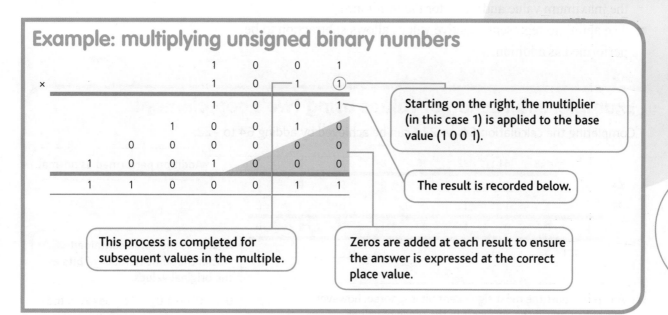

Starting on the right, the multiplier (in this case 1) is applied to the base value (1 0 0 1).

The result is recorded below.

This process is completed for subsequent values in the multiple.

Zeros are added at each result to ensure the answer is expressed at the correct place value.

Signed binary

There are alternative binary representations that can be used to represent positive and negative values.

Two's complement representation uses the inversion of a value with an additional one added to the result. This means that the most significant bit in a sequence has a negative weighting.

Key term

Two's complement binary
A modification of pure binary numbers to enable negative values to be represented.

Example: negative two's complement values

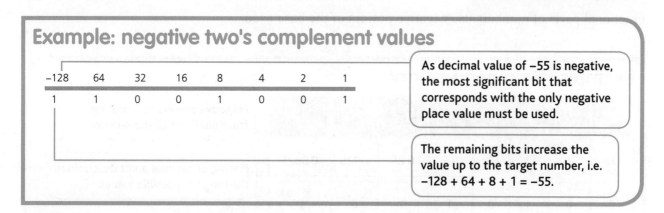

As decimal value of −55 is negative, the most significant bit that corresponds with the only negative place value must be used.

The remaining bits increase the value up to the target number, i.e. −128 + 64 + 8 + 1 = −55.

Key points:

■ The positive values (and zero) in a two's complement byte would be in the range 00000000_2 to 01111111_2 representing 0_{10} to 127_{10} inclusive.

- Negative values would be represented by 10000000_2 to 11111111_2 representing -128_{10} to -1_{10} inclusive.
- The range of values for n bits can be determined as $2^{n-1} - 1$ for the maximum value and -2^{n-1} for the minimum.
- The ability to represent negative values allows subtraction to be performed as addition.

Example: subtraction of values using two's complement

Completing the calculation $64_{10} - 22_{10}$ can be achieved by adding 64 to -22.

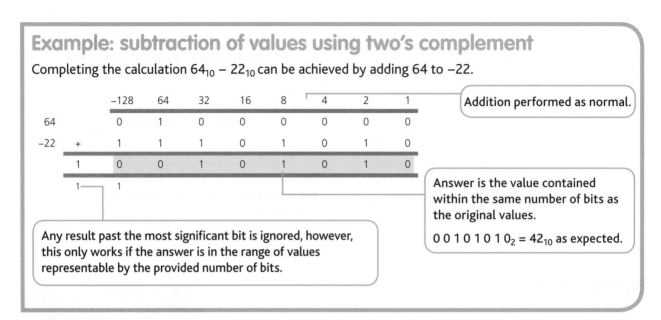

Addition performed as normal.

Any result past the most significant bit is ignored, however, this only works if the answer is in the range of values representable by the provided number of bits.

Answer is the value contained within the same number of bits as the original values.

$00101010_2 = 42_{10}$ as expected.

Numbers with a fractional part

Fractional numbers can be represented in two different forms.

Fixed point binary

Fractional parts of numbers use negative powers of the base used.

Example: fixed point binary

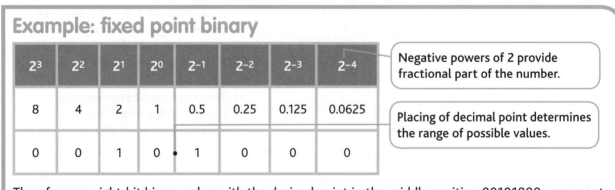

2^3	2^2	2^1	2^0	2^{-1}	2^{-2}	2^{-3}	2^{-4}
8	4	2	1	0.5	0.25	0.125	0.0625
0	0	1	0 •	1	0	0	0

Negative powers of 2 provide fractional part of the number.

Placing of decimal point determines the range of possible values.

Therefore, an eight-bit binary value with the decimal point in the middle position 00101000_2 represents the value 2.5_{10}.

Floating point binary

Key points:

- Standard form can be used to describe decimal values in terms of a **mantissa** and an **exponent**.
- The mantissa is scaled by the exponent, allowing a greater number of digits to be represented using fewer symbols.
- Floating point binary allows a limited number of bits to be used to represent wider ranging or more precise values.

Example: floating point binary

For an 8-bit floating point value with a 5-bit mantissa together with a 3-bit exponent, the decimal value of the representation 01010101_2 would be determined as follows.

Mantissa   0.1 0 1 0   Exponent   1 0 1

> The decimal point is implied here.

Both values are in two's complement form.

Step 1: Determine how much the exponent will move the decimal place.

1 0 1 = −3

Step 2: Update the mantissa.

0.0 0 0 1 0 1 0

> Move decimal place three to the left (as it is negative, positive moves to right).

Step 3: Determine the new value.

−1	0.5	0.25	0.125	0.0625	0.03125	0.015625	0.0078125
0 •	0	0	0	1	0	1	0

Value represented is equivalent to 0.078125_{10}.

Rounding errors

Key considerations:

- The limited number of bits used in fractional binary means that not all real numbers can be represented.
- For a given fractional number to be represented in binary, the fractions of the available bits must be able to be combined to produce that value.
- If this cannot be done, then the number needs to be rounded to the nearest value.
- Rounding errors can be reduced by increasing the size of the exponent, however, the size of the mantissa would have to be reduced, limiting the range of values that can be represented.

Key terms

Mantissa The part of a floating point number that describes the significant digits that make up that value.

Exponent A multiple of the base value that translates the mantissa to the order of the number that the floating point value represents.

Absolute and relative errors

Key points:

- The absolute error of a value is the difference between the value required and the value used.
  Absolute error = | value required − value used |
  (| | means we only consider the positive difference between the values.)

- The relative error is the absolute error expressed as a percentage of the target value.
  $$\textbf{relative error} = \frac{\textbf{absolute error}}{\textbf{value required}} \times 100$$

- Large magnitude values may seem to have larger absolute errors than smaller magnitude numbers.

- Relative errors are used in these cases to ascertain the error tolerance acceptable rather than an absolute value.

Normalisation of floating point form

The representation of values in standard form needs to be as efficient as possible. This is achieved by the normalisation of the mantissa to reduce repeated bits at the start of the number.

Example: normalising floating point binary numbers

Normalised floating point numbers will be in the form 0.1 or 1.0.

Any other combination can be removed by adjusting the exponent without losing the original value.

Example 1: normalising to 0.1

Consider the floating point value (in the form of a 5-bit two's complement mantissa followed by a 3-bit two's complement exponent).

The decimal point needs to be moved to the 0.1 position which is two places to the right.

0 . 0 0 1 1   0 1 1

This move reduces the exponent value required to be applied by two. The correctly normalised value is therefore:

0 . 1 1 0 0   0 0 1

Example 2: normalising to 1.0

Consider another floating point value in the same form.

1 . 1 1 0 0   0 1 0

The decimal point needs to be moved to the 1.0 position which is two places to the right.

1 . 0 0 0 0   0 1 0

This move reduces the exponent value required to be applied by two. The correctly normalised value is therefore:

1 . 0 0 0 0   0 0 0

- Should the number of bits not match the scheme chosen, an error is detected.
- This does not work if there are an even number of errors.

Majority voting

Key points:

- The same data is sent multiple times and checked together.
- Each bit is considered separately.
- The value that appears most in the same position is taken as the correct value.

Exam tip

Error detection and error correction are two different concepts. The techniques presented here only detect the presence of an error, but they do nothing to fix it. Make sure your answers in the exam do not give the impression that they do.

Checksums

Key points:

- Checksums are values that are determined separately based on the contents of a set of data.
- The checksum is sent along with the original data.
- The value is then recalculated at the receiving end to see if it matches the sent value.
- Any change to the data produces a different checksum value indicating the data sent has been corrupted.

Check digits

Key points:

- Check digits are values that are added to the end of sent data, calculated from the contents of the data.
- This value can be recalculated at the receiving end in the same way to check for the presence of errors during transmission.

Example: calculating a check digit

ISBN 10 is a common form of check digit added to the ISBN numbers of books.

Step 1: Consider the value in each position starting from 10.

ISBN

1	7	9	4	6	9	3	1	5
10	9	8	7	6	5	4	3	2

Step 2: Multiply the two values in each column.

1	7	9	4	6	9	3	1	5
10	9	8	7	6	5	4	3	2
10	63	72	28	36	45	12	3	10

Step 3: Add the results.

10 + 63 + 72 + 28 + 36 + 45 + 12 + 3 + 10 = 279

Step 4: Divide by 11 to find the remainder.

279 / 11 = 25 remainder 4

Step 5: Subtract remainder from 11 and add to end of ISBN value.

11 – 4 = 7

1	7	9	4	6	9	3	1	5	7
10	9	8	7	6	5	4	3	2	
10	63	72	28	36	45	12	3	10	

Representing images, sound and other data

Key points:

- More complex information needs different schemes to enable coding using binary values.
- Often, **data** can be represented as patterns of bits that represent key values in what is being encoded.
- Data that varies continuously over time with any value possible is considered to be analogue.
- **Signals** that are sent and received are also considered analogue if they vary in the same way as they are transmitted. At any point in time a value could be measured.
- Digital data and signals are a limited set of values that only change at distinct points in time.

When considered over a period of time, analogue data can be seen to change continuously. At any point in time a value can be measured.

For example, air pressure measured at a point in space over time would be plotted on a graph as:

Key terms

Data A collection of values that represent information in a form that is suitable to be stored and processed.

Signals The manipulation of a medium that enables the movement of data between two points.

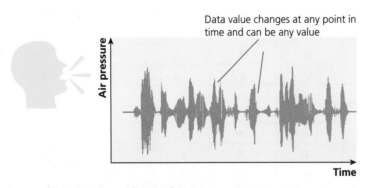

Figure 27 **What is analogue data?**

Analogue/digital conversion

Key points:

■ Computers work with discrete values that have a limited number of representations.

■ Analogue data needs to be digitised if it is to be used within a computer system.

Analogue to digital convertor (ADC)

Key points:

■ Measurements of analogue signals/data are taken at regular intervals or points using analogue sensors.

■ The closest binary approximate value is recorded based on the number of bits used per sample.

Readings are taken from an analogue sensor. They are then captured as approximate binary values.

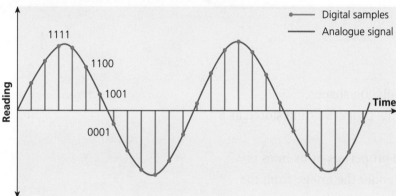

Figure 28 Analogue to digital conversion

Digital to analogue convertor (DAC)

Key point:

■ The reverse process can also be applied. For example, digital sound files are converted to analogue signals that can drive speakers to produce equivalent analogue sound waves.

Bitmapped graphics

Key points:

■ Bitmaps are the representation of analogue image data.

■ The area of an image is broken down into a distinct number of points called pixels.

■ Each of the pixels is given a colour value that is approximate to the true analogue value.

■ The storage requirement for a bitmap image can be estimated as: size in pixels × colour depth.

■ In reality, the storage requirement will be higher than this calculation gives, as image metadata will be included.

> ### Key term
>
> **Metadata** Data that describes the properties of other data. Typical metadata for images includes width and height of image, date created, location taken etc.

Example: components of a bitmap

The size of an image in pixels is determined by width × height and in this case is 10 × 10, giving an image size of 100 pixels.

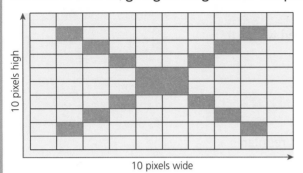

10 pixels high

10 pixels wide

This black and white example only needs a **colour depth** of 1 bit (i.e. 1 = black and 0 = white).

Resolution is expressed as the number of dots per inch (DPI) where a dot is a pixel.

Colour depth The number of bits per pixel used to provide different colours.

Render The drawing of an image based on the data provided that describes the elements within that image.

Vector graphics

Key points:

- Vector graphics are created from polygon shapes.
- Each of these objects is defined by its properties and stored as a list of data.
- The position of each object and the properties of its lines is enough to enable the computer to **render** the image from the information provided.
- The items in the list can be changed individually and the list itself has little storage overhead.
- Commonly repeated shapes are defined as primitives that form the basis for more complex graphics.

Vector graphics versus bitmapped graphics

Vector graphics are used where realism is not important and the file size should be kept down. Bitmapped graphics aim to represent images as realistically as possible.

Table 12 Vector graphics versus bitmapped graphics

Bitmap	Vector
Requires more storage space as every pixel needs to be described by a value of the same length for all instances.	Less storage needed as only the properties needed to draw the objects are required.
Less processing time required as the image only needs to be displayed as the data is presented.	More processing time required as the image has to be rendered from the properties of the objects.
Does not scale well. Stretching the image means the pixels become larger, making the image look less defined.	Scaling does not affect quality as the image is redrawn from the properties.

Digital representation of sound

Key points:

- Sound digitisation requires bit patterns to encode the changes in air pressure that caused the original noise.
- Sound as it is being digitised is **sampled** at regular time intervals.
- Values are recorded as binary patterns, the length of which is defined as the sampling resolution.
- Nyquist's theorem states that if the sampling rate used when digitising sound is twice that of the highest frequency component in the original, it will be able to be reproduced faithfully without losing any information.
- The size of a sound sample per second can be calculated as: **sample resolution × sample rate**
- This then can be multiplied by the length of a sample to find the total storage requirement.

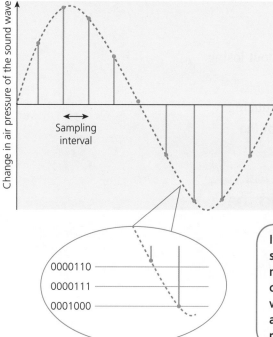

If the sample falls outside the sampling resolution, the value must be rounded up or down, changing the sound so that it will not be perfectly represented and subsequently will be reproduced inaccurately.

Figure 29 Sampling of sound

Musical Instrument Digital Interface (MIDI)

Key points:

- MIDI is a means for a computer to create predefined sounds based on the notes requested.
- For each note requested, the duration and pitch are provided so that the processing device knows what to play.

- This has the benefit of not having to encode an entire analogue sound wave to replicate it later.
- Only the information about the notes needs to be transmitted.
- The drawback is that the sound reproduced is only synthetic and lacks many of the complex frequencies found in real-world sound.

Data compression

Key points:
- Data compression is required when the storage requirements are in excess of what is available, either to store or transmit the data.
- Some types of data, such as sound and images, have parts which can be lost without an obvious effect on the quality.
- Compression can also be applied to other types of data without losing any of the original data, for example, compressing a text file to replace repeated characters with shorter reference numbers.

Lossless versus lossy compression

Lossless compression reduces storage requirements without losing any of the original data.

In comparison, lossy compression is more effective at reducing storage requirements but at the expense of losing some of the original data that will never be recovered.

Example: lossless compression techniques

Run length encoding (RLE)

This summarises patterns of data in an efficient way. So, in a sequence of 16 characters:

    AAACCCCCCGAAAGGG

RLE encoding would reduce the sequence to nine characters:

    3A6CG3A3G

> A is a repeated letter so the number of repetitions and the character are used together to reduce the storage required.

Dictionary-based methods

These replace common patterns of data with substitute tokens.

In a sequence of 33 characters:

    too wise you are, too wise you be

Dictionary-based compression reduces the sequence to 19 characters:

    1 2 3 are, 1 2 3 be

Data	Token
too	1
wise	2
you	3

Encryption

Key points:

- The process of encryption is used to obscure data so that it is unintelligible to anyone who receives it.
- The original message is considered to be **plaintext** in that it makes sense to the person writing the message.
- When encrypting, a **cipher** is used to change the message into characters that make no sense, described as **ciphertext**.
- This cipher is an algorithm that can be used both as part of encryption and, when reversed, decryption.

Encryption techniques

Key points:

- **Caesar cipher** is easily cracked as frequency analysis of the characters shows what is likely to have been substituted for common letters such as 'E'.
- **Vernam cipher** is considered perfect security for messages as the encryption has no pattern and only the key pad will help to decode the ciphertext.
- In theory, any cryptographic algorithm aside from Vernam cipher can be cracked given enough ciphertext and time.

For example, when using Caesar cipher the original message HAT becomes OHA. Characters are shifted 19 places. Therefore A becomes H, B becomes I and so on.

When the message is received, the reverse process is applied.

Key terms

Plaintext An original message to be sent in an unencrypted format.

Cipher An algorithm that changes plaintext into a format that can only be deciphered if the algorithm is known.

Ciphertext The encrypted output of plaintext determined by a specified cipher.

Caesar cipher A basic form of encryption. Letters in a message are all shifted up or down the alphabet by a defined number of characters.

Vernam cipher (or one-time pad) A more secure form of encryption. A secret random key pad, which is the same length as the message, is used to encrypt the plaintext. The pad is shared securely so only the holder can decrypt the message.

Key pad is a shared sequence of characters used in combination with the plaintext to create new ciphertext values.

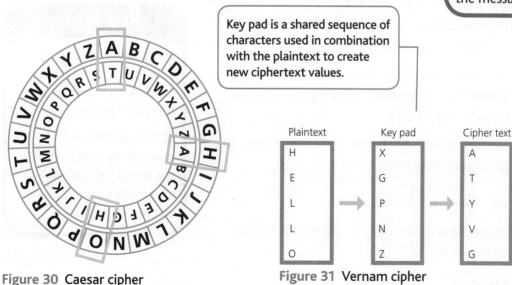

Figure 30 **Caesar cipher**

Figure 31 **Vernam cipher**

Do you know?

1 What is the principal grouping of bits within a computer referred to as?
2 What is the correct order of the number prefixes mega, tera, kilo and giga?
3 What is the decimal value of the two's complement byte 10000111?
4 What are the two components of floating point numbers?
5 What are the differences between lossy and lossless compression?
6 What is the most secure cipher possible?

2.2 Fundamentals of computer systems

You need to know

- Computer systems are the combination of hardware and software.
- Different types of software perform different roles.
- Programming languages are classified by generation.
- Turning code into executable programs involves a variety of tools.
- Logic gates form the basis of computer hardware.
- Boolean algebra can be used summarise and simplify logic circuits.

Hardware and software

A computer system is a device, or collection of devices, that can process a set of given inputs to produce required outputs.

Computer systems are the combination of hardware and software working together. Hardware cannot process any inputs or action any outputs if it is not told how to do so.

Software provides the instructions to operate system hardware in a way that produces the required outputs.

Classification of software

Software is needed to perform different roles within a computer system and is classed in two ways.

Application software

Key points:
- Application software is designed to carry out a variety of operations to achieve the user's goals.

Key terms

Hardware The physical parts of a computer that combine to form part of a computer system.

Software Data and instructions that control the computer hardware to allow it to function as a complete system.

- Typically, this is the software that enables the user to do something useful with the computer system, for example spreadsheets, word processing packages, web browsers etc.

System software

Key points:

- System software supports the running of the computer system both in terms of general operation and system maintenance.
- Users do not achieve anything with system software but it ensures the computer system operates as intended.

System software includes:

- operating systems: software that controls the running of the computer system and provides a platform to enable other software to run
- utility programs: software designed to optimise and maintain the operation of the computer system
- libraries: common program elements that can be used in other software as needed to save the programmer having to rewrite commonly used sets of operations
- translators (compiler, assembler, interpreter): software that converts programs written in a language into machine code that a computer system can execute

Role of an operating system (OS)

Key points:

- An OS acts as a platform for software to run on differing types of hardware in a consistent way, providing common services that programs can make use of.
- Software that runs does not need to know how the hardware works and it is the job of the operating system to manage this independently.
- Operating systems handle many different aspects of computer system operation.

> ### Exam tip
>
> Ensure you identify and describe the types of software in your answers rather than brands and versions of software you can buy.

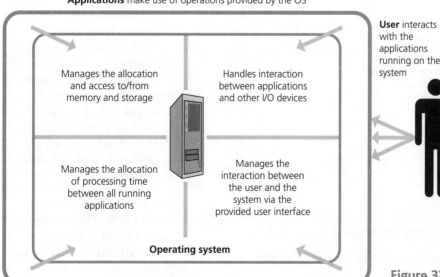

Applications make use of operations provided by the OS

Manages the allocation and access to/from memory and storage

Handles interaction between applications and other I/O devices

Manages the allocation of processing time between all running applications

Manages the interaction between the user and the system via the provided user interface

Operating system

User interacts with the applications running on the system

Figure 32 Functions of an OS

Classification of programming languages

Key points:

- Computer program instructions are represented as **machine code**, a series of 1s and 0s that the processor directly executes.
- This code is not realistically editable by a programmer but is required to instruct the processor of a computer.
- Machine code is referred to as a first-generation language, as it was the original form of computer programming.
- Second-generation languages provide a means to summarise machine code into something more understandable by humans.
- **Low-level languages** (assembly language, for example) aid the programmer by making the code easier to read, construct and subsequently edit.
- Coding happens close to the level of the processor, enabling more direct control to be applied.
- Subsequent generations of languages were designed to be closer to the understanding of programmers and how they communicate.
- **Imperative languages** use specific, ordered statements to change the state of the executing computer.
- These statements are translated into machine code that will realise these actions.
- These languages are easier for humans to write and less burdensome; however, they do not produce the most efficient code possible for a task.

Key terms

Machine code The fundamental form of computer instructions that can be directly executed by a processor.

Low-level language Language devised to substitute common machine code commands with readable mnemonics (e.g. the instruction ADD instead of the machine code 11101010).

Imperative language Generalised language with instructions that are more understandable to a human writing them than the machine code it produces.

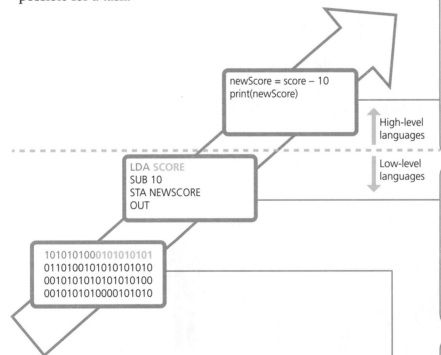

Imperative languages: statements used to describe how the state of the machine executing needs to change. Closer to human communication. Allow complex solutions to be realised more quickly, however, the resultant machine code is not as efficient as when directly coded.

Assembly language: mnemonics used for patterns of machine code to represent key commands and memory locations. Still close to machine code but easier to read by a programmer. Programs produced are still relatively difficult to follow.

Machine code: patterns of 1s and 0s that the processor understands and is able to directly execute. Difficult for a human to follow however.

Figure 33 The evolution of programming languages

Note: 'level' refers to the 'closeness' of the language to the executing processor.

Types of program translator

The translation of programming code is controlled in different ways by different types of software.

- Assembler: takes low-level assembly code and turns the represented mnemonics and labels into equivalent machine code.
- Compiler: takes high-level **source code**, optimises it as far as possible, and then produces **object code** for the target language (typically machine code that can be run on the machine that has compiled it).
- Interpreter: directly executes individual instructions contained within the source code without processing the whole of the original program.

Key points:

- Compiled programs typically execute more quickly than interpreted equivalents, however, they must first be processed as a whole which takes time and only upon completion are errors found.
- Interpreted programs only process individual lines of a program as needed, reducing up-front processing time and allowing the program to execute until instructions containing errors are attempted to run.
- The choice of interpreted or compiled programs should be made based on the intended needs and the performance profile required.
- An alternative output from a compiler can be an intermediate language, such as bytecode.
- Bytecode output is processed by a software interpreter that in turn produces the required machine code.
- Intermediate code is more **portable** than compiled code as it only needs to be formatted so that it can be processed by the target software.
- The software can then provide machine-specific low-level code.

Key terms

Source code Computer program written in a specified language by the programmer.

Object code Instructions that can be read and processed by a computer.

Portable Software or a device that can be moved and used on a number of different computer systems.

Virtual machine An emulation of a computer system.

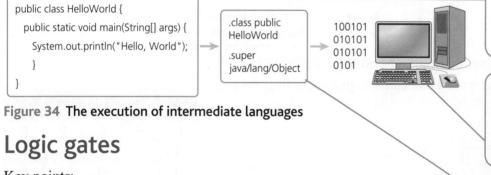

Source code produced as for any other high-level language.

Virtual machine processes intermediate code and produces equivalent machine code.

Intermediate code produced in a format that is processed by a further piece of software, typically a virtual machine.

Figure 34 The execution of intermediate languages

Logic gates

Key points:

- Logic gates are the building blocks of computer circuits.
- Different logic gates provide different outputs depending on the combinations of inputs.
- This is expressed using a truth table to outline all possible combinations of inputs and the expected outputs.

A logic gate can be expressed as a symbol or a Boolean logic symbol. The truth table shows the output for a gate based on the state of the inputs.

OR gate

$Y = A + B$

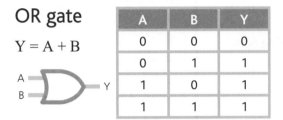

A	B	Y
0	0	0
0	1	1
1	0	1
1	1	1

AND gate

$Y = A.B$

A	B	Y
0	0	0
0	1	0
1	0	0
1	1	1

NOT gate

$Y = \bar{A}$

A	Y
0	1
1	0

XOR gate

$Y = A \oplus B$

A	B	Y
0	0	0
0	1	1
1	0	1
1	1	0

NAND gate

$Y = \bar{A}.\bar{B}$

A	B	Y
0	0	1
0	1	1
1	0	1
1	1	0

NOR gate

$Y = \bar{A} + \bar{B}$

A	B	Y
0	0	1
0	1	0
1	0	0
1	1	0

Figure 35 Common logic gates and their truth tables

Adder and half adder

Logic gates can be combined to perform more complex logic operations. For example, adding two bits together can be completed using a logic circuit called a half-adder:

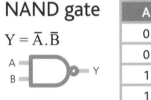

Two bits to add

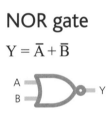

Sum of the two bits

Any carry produced from the addition

A	B	S	C
0	0	0	0
0	1	1	0
1	0	1	0
1	1	0	1

If more than single bit values need to be added, a different circuit called a full-adder can be used that can accept a carry in from a previous addition.

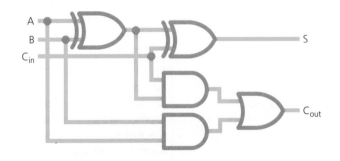

C_{IN}	A	B	S	C_{OUT}
0	0	0	0	0
0	0	1	1	0
0	1	0	1	0
0	1	1	0	1
1	0	0	1	0
1	0	1	0	1
1	1	0	0	1
1	1	1	1	1

Boolean expressions, together with brackets to force components to be evaluated sooner, can be read to construct logic circuits:

$$Y = \bar{A}.(B + C)$$

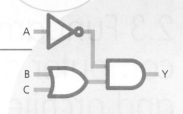

Other combinations of gates can be used for standard computer operations. Memory circuits are collections of logic circuits known as edge-triggered D-type flip-flops.

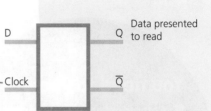

Data to store D — Q Data presented to read

Connected to system clock to synchronise the receiving and storing of data

Clock — $\bar{Q}$

Boolean algebra

Key points:

- Boolean expressions to produce intended outputs should be simplified wherever possible.
- Boolean identities can be applied to expressions to reduce the amount of logic required to realise the intended output.

Synoptic link

The use of logic gates should be considered alongside the binary representation of data as considered in Section 2.1.

Table 13 **Explanations of the main identities and rules**

A.B = B.A	The order in which two variables are ANDed makes no difference
A+B = B+A	The order in which two variables are ORed makes no difference
A.0 = 0	A variable ANDed with 0 equals 0
A+1 = 1	A variable ORed with 1 equals 1
A+0 = A	A variable ORed with 0 equals the variable
A.1 = A	A variable ANDed with 1 equals the variable
A.A = A	A variable ANDed with itself equals the variable
A+A = A	A variable ORed with itself equals the variable
$A.\bar{A} = 0$	A variable ANDed with its inverse equals 0
$A+\bar{A} = 1$	A variable ORed with its inverse equals 1
$\bar{\bar{A}} = A$	A variable that is double inverted equals the variable
(A.B).C = A.(B.C)	It makes no difference how the variables are grouped together when ANDed
(A+B)+C = A+(B+C)	It makes no difference how the variables are grouped together when ORed
A.(B+C) = A.B+A.C	The expression can be distributed or factored out, meaning that variables can be moved in and out of brackets either side of the expression. In English this expression would be A AND (B OR C) = (A AND B) OR (A AND C)

- DeMorgan's laws are special cases where inverted statements can be interchanged using different logic expressions:

$$\overline{A + B} = \bar{A}.\bar{B} \qquad \overline{A.B} = \bar{A}+\bar{B}$$

Do you know?

1 What are the two main elements of a computer system?
2 What is system software?
3 What functions do operating systems perform?
4 How are compilers used in the creation of computer programs?
5 How is an XOR logic gate different to an OR gate?
6 What are the outputs produced by a full adder?

2.3 Fundamentals of computer organisation and architecture

You need to know

- Computers are the combination of many individual components.
- Computer components work together to execute instructions stored in memory.
- The processor is central to the fetching and executing of instructions.
- Instructions are formed from opcodes and operands.
- Processor performance is affected by a range of factors.
- External hardware devices add to the functionality of a computer.

Internal hardware components of a computer

Computers are the main components within computer systems that carry out instructions and process data. Computers themselves are a collection of components. These components are housed on a main circuit board called a **motherboard**.

Table 14 **The main components of a computer**

Component	Description
Processor	The part of the computer responsible for retrieving and executing program instructions.
Main memory	An area of storage containing program instructions and data used and updated by the processor.
Address bus	A path of wires connecting key components with the processor that carries the location that data should either be sent to or read from.
Data bus	A separate path for connecting components to the processor for carrying data that needs to be transferred.
Control bus	Used by the processor and communicating components when transferring data along the data bus to provide additional information and control signals to manage the transfer.
I/O controllers	Components that manage the transfer of data between the processor and any **peripheral devices** that are connected to the computer.

Key terms

Motherboard A circuit board that provides connections between all the hardware components of a computer system.

Address An identifier that locates a specific resource in a computer so that data can be sent and retrieved from it. Typically used to identify segments of the computer's main memory.

Peripheral devices Hardware components that provide additional functionality to a computer but are not necessarily required for that computer to operate.

Example: communication via buses

In Figure 36, data is being received by the processor as captured at an I/O controller (for example, a key being pressed on a keyboard). This happens in three stages.

1 The I/O controller signals the processor via the control bus that it has data that needs collecting.

2 The address of the device where data is being read from is placed on the address bus to signal that the sending device should present the data.

3 The data to be transferred is placed on the data bus and the processor reads it.

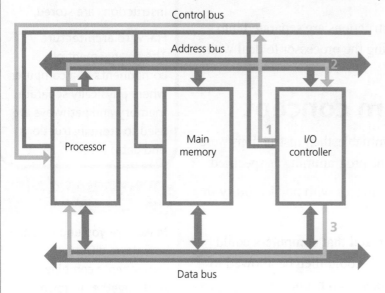

Figure 36

In Figure 37 data is being sent from the processor to be stored in main memory. This happens in three stages.

1 The address where the data is to be written is sent out on the address bus.

2 The data to be written is placed on the data bus.

3 The processor signals on the control bus that the data is to be written resulting in the addressed device (main memory) reading the data from the data bus.

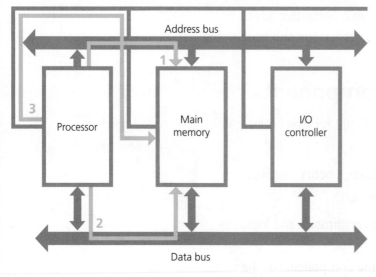

Figure 37

Key points:

- The arrangement of computer components is changeable depending on the desired operation of the machine.
- For example, main memory is typically a shared resource where program instructions and data are held together, referred to as **von Neumann architecture**.
- The shared nature of this memory means that the processor has to schedule the communication of instructions and data at separate times.
- In **Harvard architecture**, data and instructions are separated into separate memory components enabling the processor to deal with both simultaneously.

The stored program concept

Originally, computers were not reprogrammable; their instructions were hard-wired, and the machines followed the programming as specified.

This meant that computers were fixed devices with no flexibility in their purpose.

As technology developed, it was recognised that computers could store instructions in main memory which could then be allowed to change. Instructions could be adapted based on need.

Machine-code instructions that are stored in main memory are fetched and subsequently executed by the processor in the same way data is processed. Essentially instructions are treated as any other data.

Structure and role of the processor and its components

The operation of components that make up a computer has to be coordinated to achieve the execution of instructions and processing of data.

The processor and its components

The processor is the central device in a computer that coordinates and controls its operations.

Within the processor are several major components that work together to process data and instructions.

- Arithmetic logic unit (ALU): performs arithmetic and logic operations on data provided to it.
- Control unit: directs the operation of the components of the processor in response to the instructions it decodes.
- Clock: provides a regularly timed signal that is used to synchronise the operation of computer components.

Key terms

Von Neumann architecture The arrangement of components of a computer where main memory is a single shared resource where both data and instructions are stored.

Harvard architecture The arrangement of components of a computer where physically separate memory and pathways are used to store instructions and data.

Exam tip

Make sure you understand how these different components combine and work together to form computer systems.

- General-purpose **registers**: used to temporarily store data that is produced as a by-product of executing programming instructions.
- Dedicated registers: components within the processor that fulfil specific roles in its ongoing operation.

Table 15 Types of dedicated register

Dedicated register	Description
Program counter	Stores the memory location of the next instruction that needs to be executed.
Current instruction register	Holds the current instruction fetched from memory that needs to be decoded and executed.
Memory address register	Used by the processor to hold the address of where data should be read from or written to.
Memory buffer register	Holds data that is being transferred to or from the processor.
Status register	Holds flag values that indicate the operational state of the processor including any error conditions that may affect the results produced when processing.

The fetch–execute cycle

The main purpose of a processor is to receive and execute programming instructions that process data input into a computer.

Processors follow a repeated process that is responsible for collecting instructions from their stored location and deciding what actions to perform as a result.

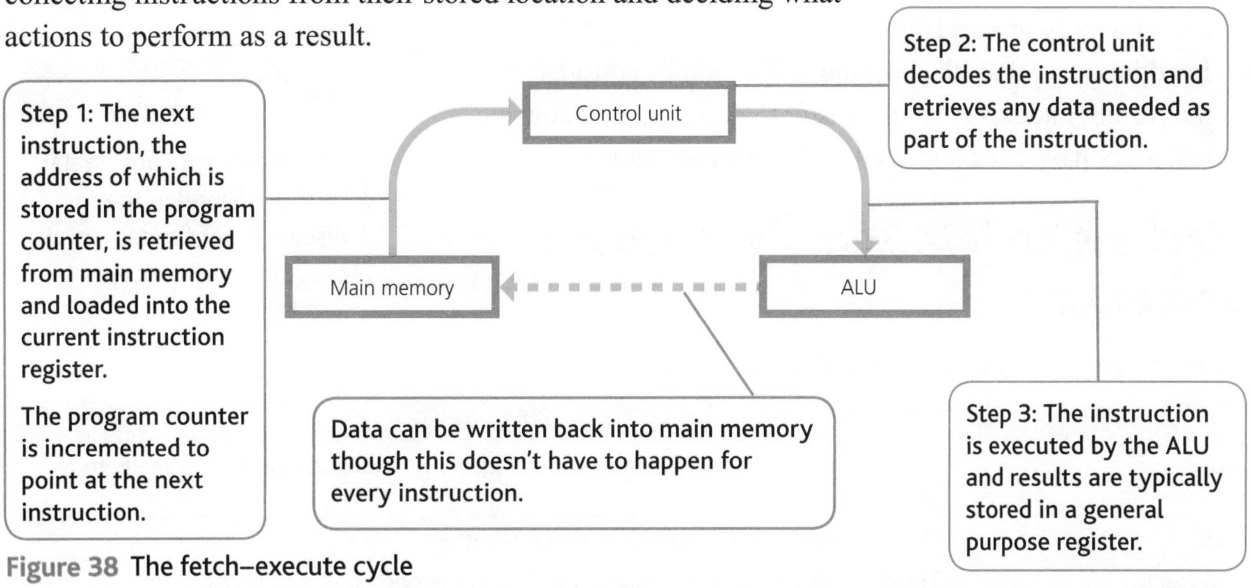

Step 1: The next instruction, the address of which is stored in the program counter, is retrieved from main memory and loaded into the current instruction register.

The program counter is incremented to point at the next instruction.

Step 2: The control unit decodes the instruction and retrieves any data needed as part of the instruction.

Control unit

Main memory

ALU

Data can be written back into main memory though this doesn't have to happen for every instruction.

Step 3: The instruction is executed by the ALU and results are typically stored in a general purpose register.

Figure 38 The fetch–execute cycle

The processor instruction set

Key points:

- For every processor there is a designed **instruction set** that specifies how the processor can be instructed in machine code.
- Different makes of processor may specify different instruction sets so it does not follow that the same machine code operates the same way in different processors.

- Instructions are constructed with two parts:
  - □ opcode: the basic machine operation that instructs the processor which operation to perform
  - □ operand: the data to be manipulated by the operand (can be a value, memory address or register).

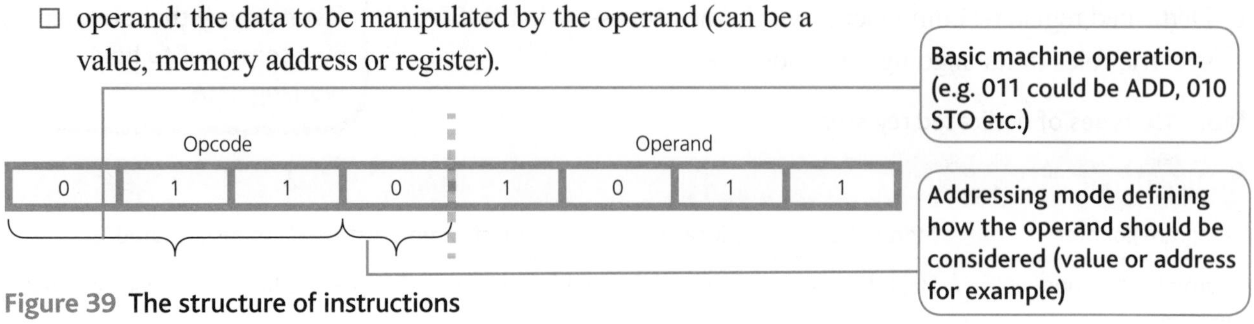

	Opcode			Operand			
0	1	1	0	1	0	1	1

Basic machine operation, (e.g. 011 could be ADD, 010 STO etc.)

Addressing mode defining how the operand should be considered (value or address for example)

Figure 39 **The structure of instructions**

Addressing mode

Key points:

- As specified in the opcode, the addressing mode defines how the operand should be used.
- When the addressing mode is set as immediate, the operand is to be interpreted as an actual value.
- In immediate mode the operand 0101 would be considered to be the value 5.
- When the addressing mode is set as direct, the operand is to be interpreted as a memory address which can refer to a location in main memory or a register.
- In addressing mode, the operand 0101 could be considered the memory address 0x5 or register r5 depending on how the resources have been allocated within the computer.

Synoptic link

These concepts are similar to those found in the discussion of fundamental programming concepts in Section 1.1.

Machine code/assembly language operations

Table 16 **Common operations that all processors execute**

Operation	Description
Load	Data is retrieved from a memory address into a general purpose register ready to be used by the ALU.
Add	Data specified in the operands is added together.
Subtract	The difference between the data specified in the operands is calculated.
Store	Move data from the processor's general purpose register into a specified memory location.
Branching	Used to change the flow of a program out of sequential order in two different ways: ■ conditional: jumps to a different instruction should the condition be met, otherwise the flow of the program continues sequentially ■ unconditional: always jumps to a specified instruction when reached.
Compare	Checks for equivalence of specified operands.
Logical bitwise operators (AND, OR, NOT, XOR)	Performs logical comparisons between operands.
Logical	Shifts the pattern of bits in an operand by a specified amount either left or right.
Halt	Stops the execution of a program.

Interrupts

Key points:

■ The processor will continue to fetch and execute instructions sequentially for a given program indefinitely.

■ Should other programs or devices require processor time, the current operation needs to be remembered and the new set of instructions started.

■ A signal called an interrupt is used to suspend the program currently being executed by the processor and a separate program called an interrupt service routine is executed.

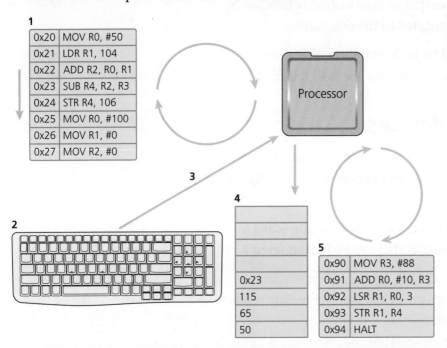

Figure 40 Servicing interrupts

Factors affecting processor performance

Processor performance is affected by:

■ The number of cores: a processor with more than one core is able to simultaneously work on multiple tasks.

■ The amount of cache memory: more cache means that main memory does not have to be accessed as frequently, which can slow down the transfer of data.

■ Clock speed: the faster the processor clock runs, the more operations can be completed in one second, because the leading edge of the clock pulse is used as a trigger to activate circuitry.

■ Word length: a greater word length enables the processor to handle more data per instruction, improving the performance of data-intensive applications.

Exam tip

You will be required to understand and apply the operations of simple low-level programs (as in Table 16). Gain experience of writing assembly-language programs either directly or using a simulator such as Little Man Computer (though recognise that instruction sets vary and do not directly reflect that found in the exam).

1 Program runs sequentially as controlled by the fetch–execute cycle.

2 Key pressed on keyboard and needs to be actioned.

3 Interrupt signal sent to processor.

4 Current state of registers and next instruction to continue with stored on a stack.

5 Interrupt service routine associated with interrupt received completed to handle the event that caused the interrupt.

Once completed, the previous register values and location of next instruction restored.

Key term

Cache memory Small amounts of fast access memory used as a store of regularly used data/instructions to reduce the need for the processor to retrieve from slower main memory.

- Address bus width: an increase in width enables more memory addresses to be used, resulting in the processor being able to access more main memory locations.
- Data bus width: an increase in width allows more data to be transferred to and from the processor in one cycle, reducing time waiting when transferring large amounts of data.

External hardware devices

Computers process data according to the instructions provided. The collection of data and the output of information is handled by external peripheral devices connected to the computer.

External devices are compared by understanding their main characteristics, purposes and suitability for the task required.

Input and output devices

Input devices are hardware components external to the computer that capture data and control signals and present them in a digital form suitable for processing.

For example, a barcode reader is a device that optically scans a barcode to determine a code number that can be looked up in a database.

- Scanning is automatically performed and the user merely needs to point the reader at the barcode.
- Barcode readers are suitable for entering code numbers accurately and quickly without the need for a user be involved in the transcription of the value.

Output devices are components that produce information or actions presented by the computer.

For example, a laser printer is a device that prints textual and graphical information on paper.

- A laser printer charges the paper and transfers powdered ink across the page producing high quality pages.
- Laser printers produce sharp images and text but are expensive.

Devices can also have both input and output features under different circumstances.

Exam tip

You should not limit yourself to learning only about the devices mentioned here. Make sure you are aware of the characteristics and use of a range of different devices.

Secondary storage devices

Key points:

- Main memory is **volatile** storage and data cannot be accessed if the computer is restarted.
- Data should be stored on non-volatile devices to be retained should the computer be powered down.
- Secondary storage devices are used for this purpose.

Table 17 Types of secondary storage devices

Type	Characteristics	Purposes	Suitability	Capacity	Speed
Magnetic hard disk	Enclosed metal disks where data is stored as differently magnetised areas.	Permanent mass storage within the case of a computer system or as a removable storage device, usually requiring a power source.	Need for own power source limits the flexibility of the device. More suited for fixed installation unless large amounts of data have to be moved.	Very large; 1 TB+ storage not uncommon.	Generally good read/write times, however, mechanical nature of device limits performance.
Optical disk	Reflective disk where data is represented by indentations on the surface. Light shined on to reflect the data pattern when read required.	Used for archiving data or transporting between computer systems.	Useful for smaller amount of data and highly portable. Generally disks are written once (though rewritable disks are available).	Limited. Blu Ray has highest capacity at 128 GB.	Slowest of the three. Disk has to spin and data throughput is slow.
Solid-state disk	NAND flash memory used with a controller that manages pages and blocks when writing. Flash memory is composed of electrical circuits that retain data when not being powered.	Used to transport files in a removable drive or as a mass secondary storage device permanently connected to the computer.	Suitable for storing data that relies on fast retrieval. Often used to improve the performance of key software installed within a computer system.	Relatively large, though magnetic disks offer more storage at a cheaper price.	Closer to main memory access speeds as the device stores data electronically.

Do you know?

1 What are the three buses that connect the components of a computer?

2 What is the stored program concept?

3 What dedicated registers are found within a computer processor?

4 What are the four main stages of the fetch–execute cycle?

5 What are the components of computer instructions?

6 How does increasing the clock speed of a processor improve its performance?

2.4 Consequences of uses of computing

You need to know

- Developments in computer science have dramatically reshaped societies.
- Those that develop computing systems and communications technologies have great power to make change happen.
- The responsibility on developers is influenced by many different issues.
- The scale of reach of digital technology produces global concerns.

Individual (moral), social (ethical), legal and cultural issues and opportunities

The advances in computer science and digital technologies have had a profound impact on society, both on an individual level and also on a global scale.

These impacts have been both positive and negative and future developments will provide many opportunities and risks.

Types of opportunities and risks include:

- moral: consideration of individual behaviour and what is developed as a person's concept of what is right or wrong
- ethical: the way society attempts to define a set of moral values and principles that is deemed acceptable and right
- legal: definitions by law of what is considered right and wrong for the country passing and enforcing laws
- cultural: factors that influence the beliefs, attitudes and actions of people within a society.

Exam tip

Questions based on this section are likely to have high marks and will require extended written responses. Make sure you are able to plan your answers in a logical and clearly presented manner.

Communication and information flows

The rise of the internet has enabled interconnected communication on a massive scale globally. Data about individuals is easy to collate and summarise in any way imaginable.

There is now the capacity to:

- monitor behaviour: the habits of users of digital devices can be recorded, often without the user being fully aware or in ways they would not consider
- amass and analyse personal information: the collation of information about users enables the holders to use the data for means that might not otherwise be possible and on a scale that involves wider sections of society
- distribute, publish, communicate and disseminate personal information: information is a commodity that has value, so the collation of as much data as possible will always have value to those collecting it.

Controllers of technology

Key points:

- Computer scientists and software engineers are the 'gate-keepers' of this information and therefore have great power and responsibility.
- The software and algorithms they produce embed moral and cultural values.
- Legal and societal considerations will influence the choices that these developers make.
- The wide-reaching nature of technology across the whole world creates great potential for any number of individuals.
- There is potential for massive benefits to society, but also the danger of great harm.

Legal considerations

In an attempt to define what is legal in terms of computer use in the UK, there are specific Acts of Parliament that define acceptable computer and digital technology use.

- The Data Protection Act: defines what is acceptable in the collation and use of an individual's personal data. Data collected must:
  - ☐ be processed lawfully
  - ☐ be processed only for the use intended
  - ☐ be relevant for the purpose intended
  - ☐ be accurate
  - ☐ be kept up to date
  - ☐ not be kept longer than necessary
  - ☐ be kept securely
  - ☐ not be transferred to other countries without adequate protection

- The Freedom of Information Act: gives individuals the right to access data recorded about themselves by public bodies.
- The Computer Misuse Act: is aimed at preventing the use of a computer for unauthorised access and subsequent misuse of other systems. It states that there must be no unauthorised:
  - ☐ use of computer programs or data
  - ☐ access with further criminal intent
  - ☐ modification of computer material

Do you know?

1 What is the difference between moral and ethical considerations?
2 What is used to define what is considered right and wrong in a country?
3 Why do businesses want to collect personal data on a massive scale?
4 Who, ultimately, has a moral duty for the ethical development of software?
5 Which UK Act of Parliament defines the acceptable use of personal data?
6 What enables an individual to gain access to public records kept about them?

2.5 Fundamentals of communication and networking

You need to know

- Computer systems can be connected to share data.
- Networks of computers can be arranged in different ways.
- Computers on networks can perform different roles to facilitate operations required.
- Network interconnections can be both wired and wireless.
- The internet is the world's biggest network.
- Protocols define the rules of electronic communication.

Communication

The connection of two computer systems must establish the method and processes by which communication will take place.

Communication methods

Key points:

- Transmission methods can either be **serial** or **parallel**.
- Data transmission can be controlled by using a timing signal such as a clock.
- Synchronous transmission sends data in blocks while sharing a clock signal.
- The data is commonly sent on the leading edge of a clock pulse so that the receiving device knows when data is being sent.
- Asynchronous data transmission occurs without a clock. Instead, start and stop bits mark the length of the frame of data being sent.
- The receiving device begins listening once a start bit is received and ends once the stop bit is subsequently received.
- Data is read at predetermined intervals by the receiving device using its own internal clock.

Key terms

Serial Communication that's processed in individual components, one at a time.

Parallel Communication where multiple parts of a message are sent at the same time.

Comparison of serial and parallel transmission

Parallel transmission occurs when data is sent simultaneously along different lines or channels.

More data can be transferred in one cycle. However, data needs to arrive at the same time, limiting the frequency that communication can be allowed to take place in order to guarantee this.

Parallel links are subject to 'crosstalk' (interference) when running at higher frequencies.

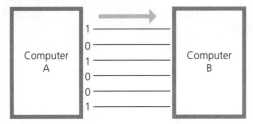

Figure 41 Parallel transmission

Serial transmission occurs across a single wire or channel by sending each part separately.

While the amount of data moved in one cycle is minimal, serial connections can be run at much higher frequencies, resulting in an overall greater data throughput than parallel.

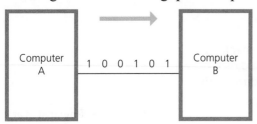

Figure 42 Serial transmission

Communication basics

Table 18 Fundamental considerations for all methods of communication

Concept	Description
Baud rate	The rate at which information is transmitted across a communication channel, measured as symbols per second.
Bit rate	The rate at which data (as bits) is transmitted.
Bandwidth	The amount of data that can be transmitted across a channel at any one time.
Latency	Any measured delay in the receiving of transmitted data from when it was sent.
Protocol	A set of rules that communicating devices follow to ensure the accurate sending and receiving of messages.

Key points:

■ Baud rate is a measure of symbols being sent.
■ A symbol could consist of multiple bits, hence the baud rate will always be equal to or lower than the bit rate.
■ Bit rate is directly proportional to bandwidth.
■ As more bandwidth is made available, so the number of bits that can be sent increases.

Networking

Networks connect groups of computers together with the purpose of sharing data and resources.

Network topology

Key points:

■ The arrangement of computers and network hardware is defined as its topology.
■ Physical topologies describe the actual physical arrangement of the devices on the network.
■ A physical star topology is arranged with a common network point in the centre where devices are connected.

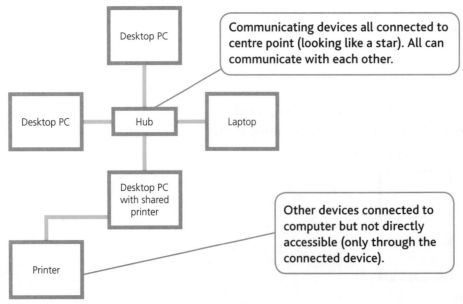

Figure 43 Physical star topology

- Logical topologies define how devices on the network communicate.
- Logical topologies do not always reflect the physical arrangement.
- Physical topologies can behave in a different manner logically.

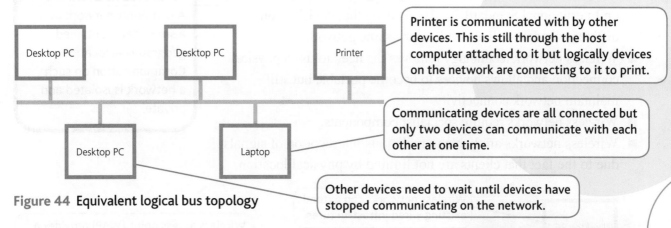

Printer is communicated with by other devices. This is still through the host computer attached to it but logically devices on the network are connecting to it to print.

Communicating devices are all connected but only two devices can communicate with each other at one time.

Other devices need to wait until devices have stopped communicating on the network.

Figure 44 Equivalent logical bus topology

Types of networking between hosts

Key points:

- The role of communicating devices on a network is decided based on the level of control required by individual machines and the method of maintaining the network.
- In a **peer-to-peer** network, all **hosts** have equal status.
- Each host decides what it shares and who it specifies has access.
- Accounts are managed per machine so each host needs to be individually configured and any changes made across the network need to be done on all clients separately.
- There is no centrally controlled storage in a peer-to-peer network so files have to be shared to be available elsewhere.
- In a **client–server** network, most computers are nominated as clients.
- There are other computers on the network that act as servers to provide services specifically for the clients on the network in a centralised manner.
- Clients request services from the servers, for example access to user files provided by a file server or access to email mailboxes from an email server.
- Management of the network can be controlled centrally via the servers as all clients have to authenticate on the network against information held on the servers.
- Client–server networks are easier to manage centrally but take longer to set up than peer-to-peer ones.

Wireless networking

Key points:

- Network interconnections can be formed from wired and/or wireless connections.

- Wireless **local area networks** can utilise technology adhering to different standards of equipment and transmission.
- For a network to be considered a WiFi network it should be based on International Standard 802.11 ensuring that devices from different vendors will all work on the same network.
- Wireless network technology removes the need to use a physical connection and allows devices to become portable but still maintain network connectivity.
- Wireless networks require specialist components.
- Wireless networks are liable to malicious interception of signals due to the fact that clients are not limited by physical location.

> ### Key term
>
> **Local area network**
> A computer network over a small, self-contained geographical location. Communication on such a network is isolated and private.

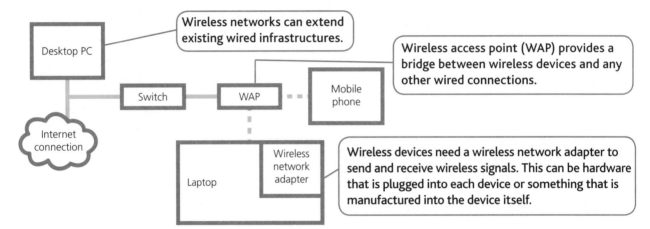

Figure 45 Wireless network

Security measures on wireless networks include:

- WPA/WPA2 (WiFi Protected Access): sophisticated encryption of data when transmitted wirelessly together with the authentication of users on the network
- SSID (service set identifier) broadcast disabled: the identifier of the wireless network is hidden so only those that know the exact name can gain access (as opposed to open broadcast to facilitate connection of devices)
- MAC (Media Access Control) address whitelisting: list of MAC addresses of wireless network adapters that are allowed on the network; all others are rejected by default.

> ### Key term
>
> **SSID (service set identifier)** A label that identifies a wireless network.

Key points:

- Devices on wireless networks cannot communicate on the same channel at the same time.
- To control the sending and receiving of data with multiple devices, CSMA/CA (carrier sense multiple access/collision avoidance) can be used.

- CSMA/CA works by:
  - ☐ the sending device checking the channel it is connected to for the presence of other communication
  - ☐ if the channel is busy, it waits a random amount of time before trying again
  - ☐ if the channel is clear the data is sent.
- Request to send/clear to send (RTS/CTS) may also be optionally used, where the wireless access point receives an RTS request from a sending client.
- This is followed by a CTS message sent back indicating that the access point is ready to receive the transmission.

The internet

The internet is the biggest computer network in the world that connects all manner of devices.

The structure of the internet and how it works

Key points:

- The internet is a combined 'network of networks' that is not privately owned.
- Access to the internet is controlled by internet service providers (ISPs) and other large organisations that connect their networks directly to others.
- These significant contributors form the **backbone** of the internet to which other smaller networks connect.
- **Internet registries** are responsible for managing and registering internet resources within a particular area of the world.

Physical connections

Key points:

- Hardware devices called **routers** connect networks to one another.
- Routers are responsible for keeping records of connected networks that can locate a specified destination.
- More widely across the internet backbone, core routers maintain routes between principal locations.
- Routers move packets of data on to other routers until they reach their destination in a process known as packet switching.
- The flexible structure of the internet ensures there are multiple routes for each packet of data to take.
- Not all connections on the internet use the same **protocol** and, where this happens, devices called **gateways** handle the translation between the networks.

> ## Key terms
>
> **Backbone** Major data routes between key points within the internet.
>
> **Internet registry** Organisations that manage the allocation of internet resources within a geographical region.
>
> **Router** A network device that controls communication between different networks.
>
> **Protocol** A set of rules that communicating devices on a network use to ensure communication can take place in the correct format.
>
> **Gateway** A device on the edge of a network that enables communication between networks using differing protocols and media.

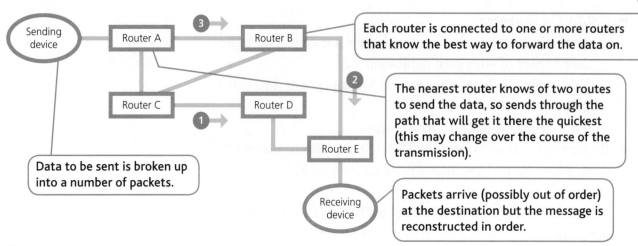

Each router is connected to one or more routers that know the best way to forward the data on.

The nearest router knows of two routes to send the data, so sends through the path that will get it there the quickest (this may change over the course of the transmission).

Data to be sent is broken up into a number of packets.

Packets arrive (possibly out of order) at the destination but the message is reconstructed in order.

Figure 46 Packet switching

Packets are assembled from chunks of the original data together with a header and footer to provide information of where to send the data and which part the packet represents.

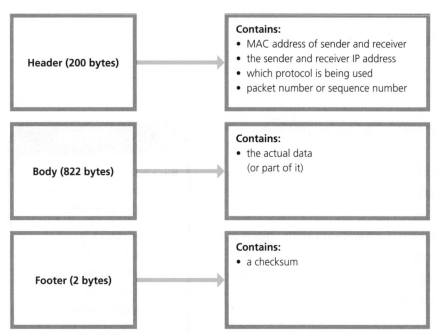

Header (200 bytes)

Contains:
- MAC address of sender and receiver
- the sender and receiver IP address
- which protocol is being used
- packet number or sequence number

Body (822 bytes)

Contains:
- the actual data (or part of it)

Footer (2 bytes)

Contains:
- a checksum

Figure 47 The contents of a typical packet of data (1 kB in this case)

Resource location

Key points:
- A URI (uniform resource identifier) is a string of characters that provides a reference to locate a resource.
- A URL (uniform resource locator) is an identifier that specifically finds resources on the World Wide Web for example: http://www.gov.uk/paye.html identifies the hostname 'www.gov.uk' where the resource 'paye.html' can be located using the 'http' protocol.
- At the base of all resources on the internet is an IP address which is an identifier for every device connected to the network.
- IP addresses are not user-friendly and instead domain names are used as aliases.

> **Key term**
>
> World Wide Web The interlinked collection of documents and resources accessible via the internet.

- Resources are located from records entered on to domain name system (DNS) servers.
- The structuring of domains is hierarchical.
- Top level domains such as .com or .org are maintained as referring servers to child domains and are the first domains that handle DNS queries.
- Domains underneath these are recorded by these servers so that requests can be directed appropriately until the authoritative server for the FQDN is found and the appropriate IP address resolved.
  1 Request to find IP address of the FQDN www.hodder.com, so the computer asks the nearest DNS server.
  2 Top level domain in FQDN is .com so request is referred to that server.
  3 .com knows where hodder.com is so request is referred on.
  4 Device with hostname www in domain hodder.com is recorded on this server so the IP address is sent back to the original client.

Key term

FQDN (fully-qualified domain name) The complete domain location of a specific resource within the DNS.

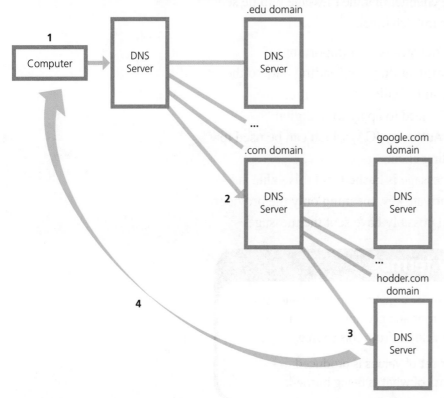

Figure 48 Using domain names

Internet security

As the internet is a publicly accessible network, devices using it should employ a range of security measures.

At the connection to the internet, a network could deploy a firewall that can use the following security methods:

- packet filtering: packet headers are checked for the type of content they say is in a packet and reject it if that type is not allowed on the network

Synoptic links

Threats to network security raise many interesting ethical and moral discussions which tie in with the principles covered in Section 2.4.

The concept of encryption is covered in more detail in Section 2.1.

- proxy servers: act on behalf of private network clients to provide access to the internet protecting them from direct exposure
- stateful inspection: examines the contents of packets to determine if they are part of a valid communication chain with an internal client.

Sensitive traffic across the internet should be encrypted. Techniques include:

- symmetric encryption: a secret key applied to messages that only the communicating devices know about
- asymmetric encryption: clients on the network make public encryption keys available so that data received encrypted with these keys can only be decrypted with a paired private key.

In any encrypted communication, the decryption key must be exchanged first. This transfer itself is a security risk.

Keys can be transferred either:

- in-band: sent across the same channel that the message will be sent
- out-of-band: sent across a separate channel.

The validity of communicating devices is also important to establish. Clients need to be confident they are sending data to the place they are expecting. This can be validated by using:

- digital certificates: individuals need to apply for a digital certificate from a **Certificate Authority** (CA) which can be used to prove the identity of the sending client
- digital signature: the entire message is **hashed** and this value is encrypted with the sender's private key, meaning only the provider of the paired public key could possibly have sent the message.

Key terms

Certificate Authority A company or organisation that validates the identity of nodes on the internet and provides electronic certification to validate communication from this source.

Hashing An identifying value or set of values is produced algorithmically from the contents of what is being hashed.

Table 19 Threats to devices sending and receiving across the internet

Threat	Description
Worms	Self-replicating malware that spreads without user interaction via the vulnerabilities of software used on computer systems.
Trojans	Malicious code hidden inside legitimate-looking sources that trick users into executing it.
Viruses	Malware that causes damage on a computer once executed.

The effects these threats pose can be reduced by:

- improved code quality: developing and testing software thoroughly so that it does not have vulnerabilities that can be exploited
- monitoring: software on the system can be used to check its operation to detect the presence of malware
- protection: anti-malware software can check programs as they are executed to see if they match the profile of known malicious software definitions.

The transmission control protocol/internet protocol

The transmission control protocol/internet protocol (TCP/IP) is the most commonly used networking protocol and the one that is used for communicating across the internet.

Features of TCP/IP

There are four layers of the TCP/IP stack.

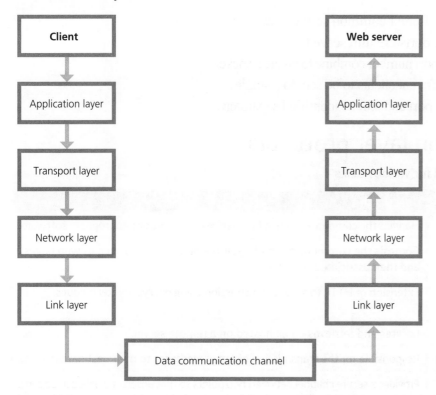

Figure 49 TCP/IP layers

Each layer performs a different role in the communication process.

- Application layer: ensures that data sent is in a consistent format as expected by the receiving device (for example, a web page would be transmitted via the conventions specified in **HTTP**).
- Transport layer: breaks apart the data to be sent and ensures that the order of the parts is maintained.

Key term

HTTP (Hypertext Transfer Protocol) Application protocol that controls the sending and receiving of World Wide Web resources.

■ Network layer: records the **IP address** of both the sending and receiving devices so that they are able to locate one another across the network.

■ Link layer: interacts with the physical medium by which the communication will travel, adding hardware **MAC addresses** so that traffic can be directed appropriately.

Key points:

■ In addition to IP address information, data packets specify the **port** that the receiving device should be listening on.

■ Applications running on the receiving device listen on a particular port, knowing that data specified for that port is intended for them.

■ The sending device can therefore know where the data is to be sent.

■ There are several well-known ports that are regularly used in network communication and are specified in the range 0–1023.

■ Specific examples of well-known ports include:
  □ Port 80 – HTTP   □ Port 22 – SSH
  □ Port 53 – DNS   □ Port 110 – POP3

■ Ports above 1023 are free to use as client ports for private network purposes.

■ Below port 49152, ports that different common services use are reserved and above this value, ports are unreserved.

■ The destination IP address and port number combine to create a socket.

■ Sockets allow requests from different clients to be sent to a single device listening on a particular port and still be identified separately.

Key terms

IP address A combination of numerical values used to identify nodes logically on a network.

Media access control address (MAC address) Hardware address of communicating device on a network.

Port A number used by a receiving device on a network where specific communication should be sent and that the receiving device will listen for.

Standard application layer protocols

Table 20 **Common protocols used for various tasks**

Protocol	Description
FTP (File Transfer Protocol)	Handles the communication of files between clients using appropriate software.
HTTP (Hypertext Transfer Protocol)	Controls the communication of hypermedia documents such as web pages and their associated resources.
HTTPS (Hypertext Transfer Protocol Secure)	Extension of HTTP to secure transmission using encryption techniques.
POP3 (Post Office Protocol (v3))	Locates and retrieves email hosted on a remote server.
SMTP (Simple Mail Transfer Protocol)	Responsible for the transmission of email messages to their destination.
SSH (Secure Shell)	Provides a secure channel between two points so that unsecured data can be sent.

Transferring files via FTP

FTP software needs to fulfil two roles:

■ server: controls access to the area where files can be transferred to and from

■ client: authenticates with the server using passwords (or anonymously if allowed) to be able to control the flow of files.

Once clients are authenticated, file transfer happens in much the same way that operating systems manage files.

Uses of Secure Shell (SSH)

Key points:

- SSH uses a client–server model.
- An SSH server is run on the target machine and listens for connections from clients.
- When connections are established, communication is encrypted using public key encryption and access is granted to effectively log on to the host machine.
- The client can run commands as if they were logged on locally at the host machine and manage the system as normal.
- The connection can also act as a tunnel allowing any data to be sent through it.

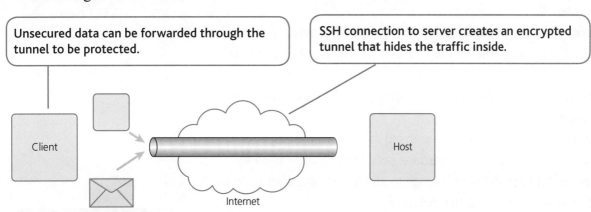

Unsecured data can be forwarded through the tunnel to be protected.

SSH connection to server creates an encrypted tunnel that hides the traffic inside.

Client

Internet

Host

Figure 50 SSH tunnelling

Retrieving and sending email

Key points:

- Email is handled using dedicated servers.
- The IP address of an email server is recorded in the domain records so that all email sent to that domain can be forwarded correctly.
- As email is received, it is stored in appropriate mailboxes ready for clients to retrieve.
- Clients use software or web interfaces to access the email on the server.
- If an email is to be sent, the server is responsible for sending the data on its way to the appropriate domain listed in the email address.

Accessing websites

The process of accessing a web page on a client involves several steps.

1 Web page is requested by client.
2 Web server responds by sending the web page as its textual form.

3 Web page is rendered within browser.

4 Other resources on the page have to be fetched in the same way so they can be added to the rendered document.

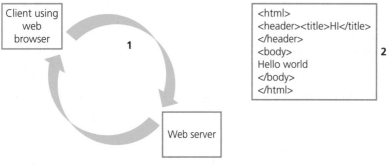

Figure 51 **Accessing web pages**

IP address structure

Key points:

- IP addresses are needed to identify devices on a network.
- If an IP address is known then packets of data can be addressed and sent.
- Typically, IP addresses are constructed from four **octets** of binary data separated by full stops.
- These values are usually summarised as decimal values.
- IP addresses consist of two parts, a network identifier used to label the network the host belongs to and a host identifier used to differentiate the host on that network.

Figure 52 **An IP address is constructed from four octets separated by full stops**

Consecutive octets are used to identify the network and host identifiers.

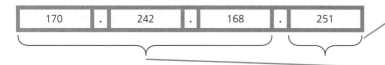

Figure 53 **An IP address is usually expressed as decimal values**

Subnet masking

Key points:

- Subnet masks are used to distinguish where the network identification portion of an IP address ends and where the host identifier begins.

> **Key term**
>
> **Octet** A group of 8 bits.

> Device with this address would therefore be host 251 on network 170.242.168.0

> Network identified as 170.242.168.0

> **Synoptic link**
>
> The conversion of values uses the same principles as binary data representation as described in Section 2.1. Understanding the bit structure of IP addressing helps to understand how subnet masks work.

- Masks do not need to use whole parts of octets, though this is the most common approach.
  For example, if an IP address 186.12.109.200 has a subnet mask of 255.255.255.0 this would mean that the network identifier is 186.12.109.0.
- Subnet masks can be specified that are partial values of an octet.

Example: subnet masking

The subnet mask 255.255.255.128 would be represented in binary as shown below.

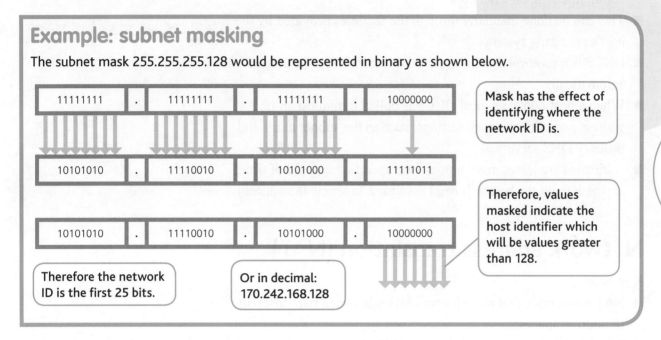

IP standards

Key points:
- The limited number of values possible for version 4 IP addresses (2^{32} = 4,294,967,296) has meant that a newer standard of IP address is required.
- IP version 6 (v6) uses hexadecimal numbers separated by colons, for example: 2321:0FF0:1238:DBB0:0033:1111:2222:AB14
- IP v6 enables the use of a wider range of addresses ensuring that there are enough addresses for all devices connected to the internet.

Public and private IP addresses

Key points:
- Not all IP addresses are routable across the internet.
- Certain ranges are prohibited from being processed by routers.
- Private IP addresses are used within private networks that do not directly need internet access (but can use other services to achieve this).
- The ranges of private IP addresses are:
  - ☐ 10.0.0.0 to 10.255.255.255
  - ☐ 172.16.0.0 to 172.31.255.255
  - ☐ 192.168.0.0 to 192.168.255.255

Dynamic host configuration protocol (DHCP)

Key points:

- IP addresses of hosts need to be configured prior to communicating on a network.
- This can be done manually through the facilities provided by the host's operating system.
- DHCP is a protocol that allows this configuration to be carried out automatically.
- When a host boots, its local DHCP is polled to request an IP address and other network settings, such as the subnet mask and primary DNS servers.
- Addresses are leased from a pool for a specified amount of time, at which point the host will need to request to renew the address or ask for a new one.

Network address translation (NAT)

Key points:

- NAT is a service that provides translation between two different IP address spaces.
- Typically NAT is used to share one public-facing IP address with a fully private network space.

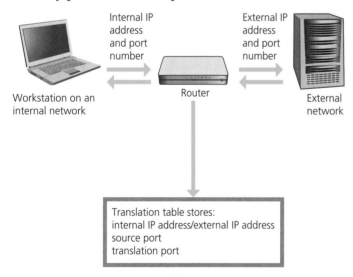

Figure 54 Network address translation

- The NAT server records the requests from private clients and refers communication to the destination with itself as the return address.
- Once data is sent back, the NAT server forwards the data back to the client who originally requested the data.

Port forwarding

Key points:

- The utilisation of NAT on a network means that services hosted on an internal network cannot be accessed directly.
- Port forwarding works on the edge of the network to relay traffic to an appropriate server hosted on a private network.
- Rules are defined that, should requests be received on a particular port, the packets are automatically forwarded to an internal IP address.

  For example, a web server might be configured inside a private network and a router at the edge of the private network connecting to the internet. The router would have to be configured to forward traffic containing destination port 80 to the server.

Client–server model

Client–server models provide a central means of control on a network.

Clients on the network make requests to use services provided by machines designated as servers. Servers respond to each request as appropriate.

Websocket protocol

Key points:

- Websocket provides a persistent connection between a client and server, removing the need for a request/response cycle initiated by the client.
- Data can be sent as **full-duplex** allowing the server of a web page to refresh elements as and when they change.
- Initially, the connection is established as a HTTP request through port 80.
- This connection establishes the two-way communication channel which allows either device to send data.
- As the communication cycle finishes, either side closes the connection.

> ### Key term
>
> **Full-duplex**
> Communication between two points that happens in both directions simultaneously (as opposed to half-duplex where only one node can communicate at one time).

CRUD and REST

Client–server interaction involves common communication principles.

The acronym CRUD summarises the functions of persistent storage, typically used to describe the operations of a database.

- Create: adds a new data object into storage.
- Retrieve: finds and reads a stored data object.

■ Update: finds a data object and updates a specified part of it.
■ Delete: removes the specified data object from storage.

Relational databases conform to the CRUD standard meaning that SQL statements can map directly to these operations:

■ Create is INSERT
■ Retrieve is SELECT
■ Update is UPDATE
■ Delete is DELETE

Representational state transfer (REST) or RESTful web services are designed to use HTTP requests to carry out CRUD operations:

■ Create uses the HTTP request POST
■ Retrieve uses GET
■ Update uses PUT
■ Delete uses DELETE

Web services

Different methods can be used by web services to format data objects between servers and the clients they service.

■ JSON (JavaScript Object Notation): is written in a typical programming form.
■ XML (Extensible Markup Language): information is contained within tags.

In comparison, JSON is:

■ easier for humans to read, in the same way as high-level languages
■ provided in a more compact format
■ easier to create
■ more efficient when being **parsed** by a computer, resulting in a speed advantage.

Thin- versus thick-client computing

Key points:

■ Network infrastructure can be developed in terms of the server hardware specification or the hardware of the clients that use them.
■ **Thick-client** computing uses standard PC hardware to act as clients on the network.
■ Clients handle processing tasks themselves, only calling on network services when needed.
■ **Thin-client** computing moves the processing onto a server.
■ Clients are limited terminals that provide interaction with user sessions running on a server.

Table 21 Thick versus thin computing

Thick clients	Thin clients
Perform better where intensive processing is required whereas thin clients rely on what is provided by the server.	Utilise low-cost and basic terminals when compared with thick clients.
Do not require continuous network access.	Are easier to maintain and support.
Do not require highly specified (and therefore costly) servers.	Require persistent network connections that need to be high capacity should more intensive tasks need to be performed.

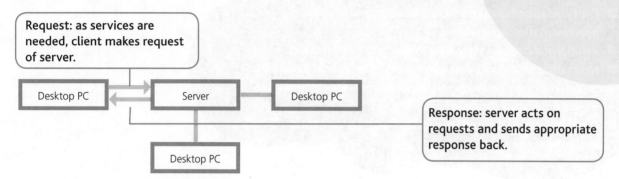

Request: as services are needed, client makes request of server.

Response: server acts on requests and sends appropriate response back.

Figure 55 Thick client computing

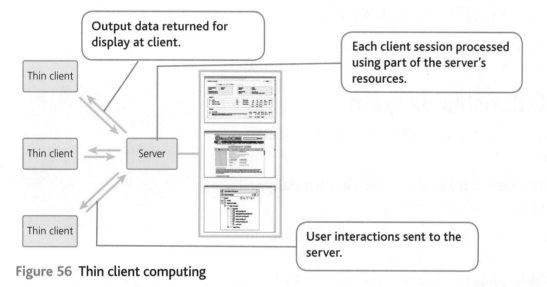

Output data returned for display at client.

Each client session processed using part of the server's resources.

User interactions sent to the server.

Figure 56 Thin client computing

Do you know?

1 Explain the differences between parallel and serial connections.

2 What is the central device used as part of a physical star topology?

3 How can wireless networks be secured?

4 What system of naming computers on a network can be used instead of referring to IP addresses?

5 Where are digital certificates obtained from?

6 What are the four layers of the TCP/IP stack?

Exam tip

Questions about this topic are likely to require you to justify the most appropriate type of network for a given scenario. Make sure your answers reflect the needs of the users in the stated scenario.

2.6 Fundamentals of databases

You need to know

- Databases are organised collections of data.
- Entity-relationship diagrams produce data models for implementation as databases.
- Relational databases store data in separate related tables.
- Normalisation reduces data redundancy in relational databases.
- Structured query language can be used to provide customisable interaction with a database.
- Databases can be designed to provide client–server access to the data.

Conceptual data models

A data model represents how sets of data are organised. They also define how they relate to one another and to properties of the real world.

Entity-relationship diagram

A school data system about pupils and their timetables could be modelled as follows.

Each distinct data object in the model is given its own entity and named appropriately, e.g. lesson, subject etc.

- Many-to-many relationship: a record of one entity is related to multiple records in another and vice versa.
- One-to-one relationship: one record of an entity is related to only one record of the connected entity.
- One-to-many relationship: one record of an entity is related to many different records of another entity (crows foot on the many side).

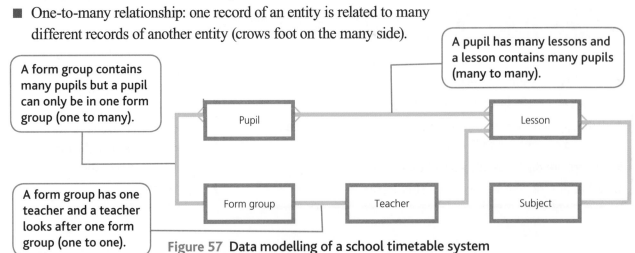

A form group contains many pupils but a pupil can only be in one form group (one to many).

A pupil has many lessons and a lesson contains many pupils (many to many).

A form group has one teacher and a teacher looks after one form group (one to one).

Figure 57 **Data modelling of a school timetable system**

Entity descriptions

Each entity can be summarised by the attributes it contains.

This is of the form: Entity Name (Attribute 1, Attribute 2, …)

From the diagram the entities could be described as follows:

- Pupil (Pupil ID, Surname, Forename, Form, Contact Name, Contact Tel)
- Lesson (Lesson ID, Subject, Date, Pupil, Room, Teacher)
- Form Group (Form Name, Teacher, Room)
- Teacher (Teacher ID, Surname, Forename, Department)
- Subject (Subject Name, Department, Key Stage)

Attributes of each entity are listed individually.

Underline indicates the attribute is used as the entity identifier that differentiates the different records within an entity.

Overline indicates the attribute is imported; it gets its value from an entity identifier within a related entity.

Relational databases

Key points:

- **Relational databases** are implementations of data models.
- Entities are realised as tables and the data in them is related as necessary by the creation of relationships.
- In some relationships, a single value **primary key** is not enough to make a record in a table unique.
- A **composite key** can be used to join two or more fields to create the key field for the table.

Key terms

Relational database Database where multiple files (tables) are linked together through predefined relationships between elements of their data. This is in contrast to a flat-file database that consists of a single file.

Primary key Unique identifier in records of a database that distinguishes data that is similar.

Composite key The combination of multiple elements of a record to ensure the key is unique for each record.

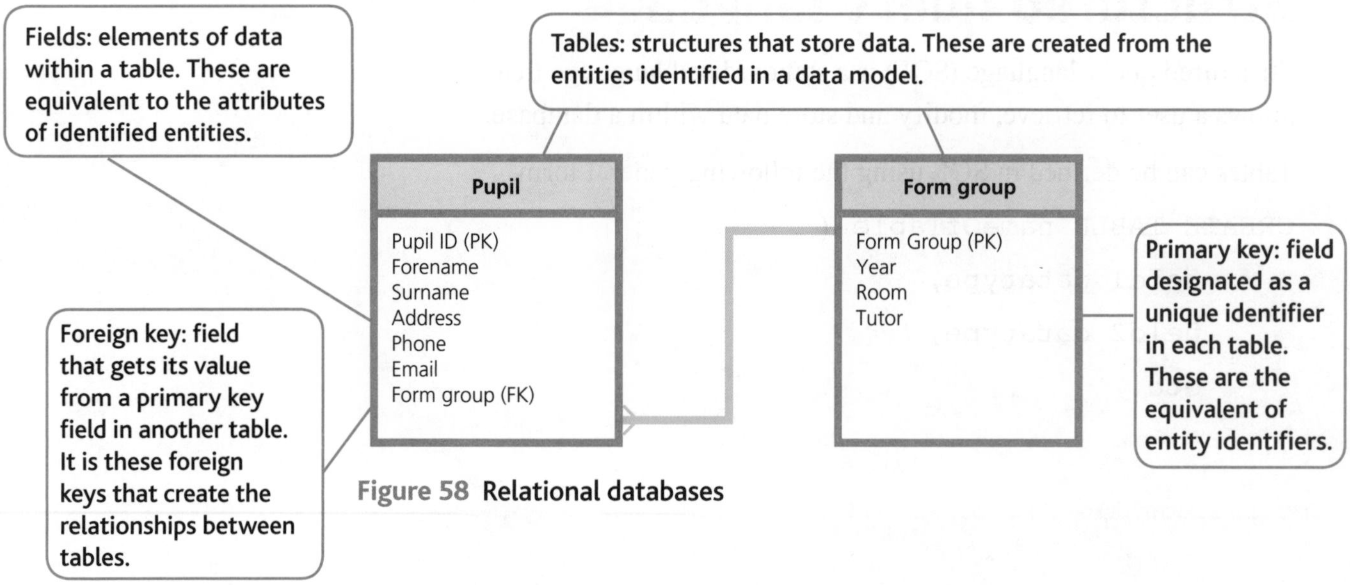

Fields: elements of data within a table. These are equivalent to the attributes of identified entities.

Tables: structures that store data. These are created from the entities identified in a data model.

Pupil
Pupil ID (PK)
Forename
Surname
Address
Phone
Email
Form group (FK)

Form group
Form Group (PK)
Year
Room
Tutor

Primary key: field designated as a unique identifier in each table. These are the equivalent of entity identifiers.

Foreign key: field that gets its value from a primary key field in another table. It is these foreign keys that create the relationships between tables.

Figure 58 Relational databases

Database design and normalisation techniques

Database normalisation is the process of rationalising related tables and fields to reduce **data redundancy** (and therefore storage space) and to improve the **integrity** of the data.

Data in the database should be reduced so that it is only ever entered once, and where relationships are used to provide duplication.

The process of normalisation follows a series of stages known as normal forms (NF). Each NF organises the database so that it meets the requirement at that stage:

■ First normal form (1NF):
  □ eliminates fields that have repeated data, for example, Items_ordered field records multiple items in an order
  □ identifies each record in the table with its own unique primary key
  □ uses a composite primary key to allow duplicate data alongside repeated data in other fields.
■ Second normal form (2NF):
  □ ensures that all fields in a table only depend on the whole of the primary key
  □ separates tables and joins them through a relationship if this is not the case.
■ Third normal form (3NF):
  □ removes **transitive dependencies**
  □ fields related to another field, which is not the primary key, removed to their own table with the related field creating a relationship.

Key terms

Data redundancy The duplication of data in multiple locations.

Integrity The accuracy of data stored measured by its correctness and how current it is.

Transitive dependency Data in a database field that is not related to the primary key that describes its record.

Structured query language

Structured query language (SQL) is a standardised language that allows a user to retrieve, modify and store data within a database.

Tables can be defined in SQL using the following general form.

```
CREATE TABLE nameOfTable (
    field1 datatype,
    field2 datatype,
    etc.
);
```

A table that stores the population of capital cities and their populations would therefore be defined as follows:

```
CREATE TABLE    cityPopulation (
    city varchar(255),
    country varchar(255),
    population int,
    PRIMARY KEY (city)
);
```

Once defined, SQL can be used to perform standard CRUD operations.

Insert (adding a data record into a table)

```
INSERT INTO cityPopulation
VALUES ("Beijing", "China", 27700000);
```

Update (change values stored in a record)

```
UPDATE cityPopulation
SET country = "Egypt", population = 24500000
WHERE city = "Cairo";
```

Select (retrieve data from a table)

```
SELECT country, population
FROM cityPopulation
WHERE city = "London";
```

Delete (remove data records from a table)

```
DELETE FROM cityPopulation
WHERE city = "Springfield";
```

Client–server databases

Databases can be provided as a networked resource allowing simultaneous access for multiple clients. If databases are used in this way, then access to data must be controlled so as not to affect the accuracy of data should multiple clients try to update the same data simultaneously.

> **Synoptic link**
>
> The client–server concept of CRUD (create, read, update and delete) was introduced in Section 2.5.

Concurrent access can be controlled by:

- record lock: as data is being accessed, it is locked to other users trying to make additional changes
- serialisation: transactions are processed individually in a serial format, not allowing multiple transactions to occur at the same time
- timestamp ordering: the time that each transaction is requested is recorded, which is then used to order the actions to carry out
- commitment ordering: prioritises commands based on the impact their completion will have on the data and other subsequent transactions

Key term

Concurrent access
Attempts made by multiple clients to access a resource at the same time.

Do you know?

1 What are the objects in data models called?
2 What are the three types of relationships that can be created in a relational database?
3 Why are databases normalised?
4 Describe the first three stages of database normalisation.
5 What are the four SQL commands that implement CRUD functions in a database?
6 How can concurrent database access be managed in a client–server database?

2.7 Big Data

You need to know

- 'Big Data' categorises data that cannot be described by standard definitions.
- It is described in terms of volume, velocity and variety.
- The vast quantities of data require processing across multiple machines.
- Functional programming is used to provide distributed solutions.
- Big Data is described as facts.
- The structure of Big Data is represented as graphs.

Concept of Big Data

Key points:

- 'Big Data' is a term used to describe data that cannot be specified in conventional terms.
- The main difficulty with processing Big Data is the lack of structure due to its size and inconsistency.
- Machine learning techniques are needed to find patterns in data and extract useful information.

Big Data is described in terms of:

- volume: the amount of data that contributes to the whole across a number of serving devices
- velocity: the rate at which data changes (often continuously)
- variety: the diversity of the sources of data contributing to an inconsistent structure

Processing Big Data

The vast volume of Big Data is spread across multiple sources and cannot be contained within a single server, therefore processing must be distributed across more than one machine.

Functional programming languages can be used to provide efficient distributed processing by supporting:

- immutable data structures: processing of data does not affect the original data, enabling multiple processes to complete separately without worrying about any side effects
- statelessness: functions called operate in isolation to ensure consistent results are produced that do not depend on the state of other processes
- higher order functions: functions are treated as objects that can be used as return values or arguments to other functions, enabling more complex results to be generated

Modelling Big Data

The complex relationships between inconsistent sources of data need to be defined.

Big Data can be described in terms of:

- fact-based models: each fact is used to capture a single piece of information
- graph schema: describes the relationships between items of information

> ### Key terms
>
> **Machine learning** Giving computers the ability to learn without having to be specifically programmed in a particular manner.
>
> **Functional programming** A programming paradigm whereby data is processed by functions that do not produce any side effects and the original data is kept as is.

> ### Synoptic link
>
> The features of functional programming are discussed in more detail in Section 2.8.

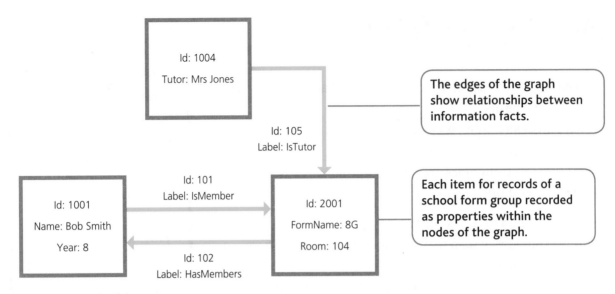

Figure 59 Modelling Big Data

Do you know?

1 How is 'Big Data' described?

2 How is the processing of Big Data distributed?

3 What type of programming language is best suited to the processing of Big Data?

4 How is Big Data modelled?

2.8 Fundamentals of functional programming

You need to know

■ Function types describe the mapping of values between domains.

■ Functions can be treated as first-class objects.

■ The application of a function applies to the arguments it is called with.

■ Composition of functions combines functions to get different results.

■ Functional programs can be realised using purely functional languages or other imperative languages with built-in support.

■ Lists are a fundamental data structure within functional programs.

Functional programming paradigm

Function type

The use of functions defines how a set of values in a domain is mapped to a second set of values in a co-domain.

A function, f, maps a set of values in the domain A to another set of values within the co-domain B such that $f: A \rightarrow B$ as can be seen in Figure 60.

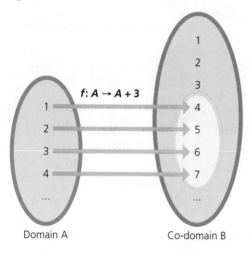

Domain A   Co-domain B

Figure 60 Functions mapping values

If a function f is defined as $f: A \rightarrow B$ then its **function type** is $A \rightarrow B$ where A is the domain and B the co-domain.

First-class object

Within functional programs, the functions themselves are treated as objects, meaning they can be used as arguments to other functions and can be used as return values in the same way as any other data type.

Table 22 Use of **first-class objects**

Use	Example from a functional program
Appear in an expression	total = total + add(2,3)
Be assigned to a variable	total = add(2,3)
Be used as arguments	total(1,add(2,3))
Be returned in function calls	return add(2,3)

Function application

Key points:
- Functions are applied to the arguments provided, e.g. add(5,2) is the function add applied to the values 5 and 2.
- The type of the function specifies the arguments and the result.
- A function taking one integer argument and producing an integer output would have the type *f: integer → integer*.
- A function taking two integer arguments and producing an integer output would have the type *f: integer × integer → integer*.
- The element *integer × integer* of this type is the **Cartesian product** of the set *integer* with itself and as such is still only one argument as it is pair, e.g. (2,3).

Partial function application

Key points:
- Function types can be specified so that functions can be returned that have only partially been applied to an argument.
- These partially applied functions can then be applied to further arguments.
- If the type of function add is defined as add: integer → (integer → integer) then add 5 returns a function that itself accepts an integer to return an integer.
- The brackets can be dropped and the function acts as if it is one function taking two arguments.

Composition of functions

Key points:
- The combination of two different functions to get a new function.
- For two functions *f:* A → B and *g:* B → C the composition *g° f* would map values from the domain A to the co-domain C.
- The output of one function is therefore used as the input to a second function, for example: if $f(x) = 2x$ and $g(y) = y^2$ then $g° f = (2x)^2$.

Writing functional programs

Functional programs can be written using:
- functional programming languages such as Haskell, Standard ML, Scheme and Lisp
- other languages such as Python, Java and C# with built-in support for creating elements of functional programs.

There are common functions that are used in functional programs.

Key terms

Function application The execution of a function using the arguments supplied to it.

Cartesian product A mathematical operation that provides a single product set from a combination of multiple sets.

Synoptic link

Cartesian products are determined from the combination of sets of values as discussed in Section 1.4.

Exam tip

As with understanding other programming languages by practising on real problems, functional programming is no different. You will be expected to read and modify simple functional programs, so you should gain experience writing solutions to problems.

Map

A function that applies a specified function to each element of a list of data.

For example, a function that doubles a given number is defined as:

```
doubleNum: integer → integer
doubleNum x = 2 * x
```

The function therefore can be applied to a single argument:

```
>> doubleNum 3
6
```

The map function can be used to apply this function to a list of values:

```
>> map doubleNum [1, 2, 3, 4]
[2, 4, 6, 8]
```

Filter

A function that processes a data structure in a specified manner to produce a new structure that matches the described condition.

The condition that controls the filtering needs to return a Boolean True or False value to be able to be used.

For example, a relational condition could be used to create a new data structure with values above a given number:

```
>> filter (>5) [1,2,6,7]
[6, 7]
```

Reduce/fold

A function that reduces a list of values into a single result by applying a specified function that combines values in some way to all elements of a list.

For example, the following applies the + operator to each element of the list starting with a value of 10. Each time the answer is applied to the next element.

```
>> reduce (+) 10 [1, 2, 3]
16
```

In some languages, a higher level of control of the folding can be afforded. In Haskell the equivalent would be:

```
>> foldl (+) 10 [1, 2, 3]
16
```

The *foldl* function applies the combining function starting with the left-most value. There is an equivalent *foldr* function that works right to left.

Lists in functional programming

Lists are a fundamental data structure used in many functional programs.

The recursive nature of functional programs benefit from lists with a *head:tail* structure where *head* is an element of the list and *tail* is another list.

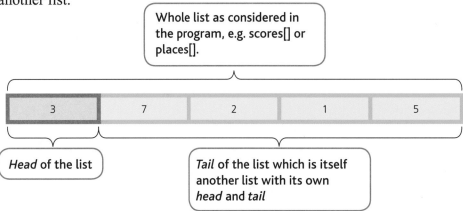

Figure 61 **List structure in functional programming**

The whole list in Figure 61 can therefore be considered as the following series of lists:

```
3:[7, 2, 1, 5]
7:[2, 1, 5]
2:[1, 5]
1:[5]
5:[ ]
```

(where [ ] is an empty list)

Table 23 **Common operations of a list**

Operation	Typical code	Result returned
Returning the head of a list	head [1, 2, 3]	1
Returning the tail of a list	tail [1, 2, 3]	[2, 3]
Testing for an empty list	null [1, 2, 3]	False
Returning the length of a list	length [1, 2, 3]	3
Constructing an empty list	let total = []	*List called total created*
Prepend an item to a list	0 : [1, 2, 3]	*List becomes [0, 1, 2, 3]*
Append an item to a list	[1, 2, 3] ++ [4]	*List becomes [1, 2, 3, 4]*

Do you know?

1 What does the function type $f: A \rightarrow B$ describe?
2 What is a first-class object?
3 What can first-class objects be used for?
4 What is the combination of two separate functions to produce a new function known as?
5 What function enables a specified function to be applied to all elements of a list?
6 What are the two component parts of a list?

2.9 Systematic approach to problem solving

You need to know

- Software development follows a range of different stages.
- Problems must be identified and analysed before being solved.
- The design of a solution is based on prior analysis.
- Designs are implemented as solutions.
- Solutions will need to be tested and evaluated.

Aspects of software development

Key points:

- Software development can take place using differing **methodologies**, each with their own processes and means of reaching a final software product.
- There are common stages that most methodologies employ in some form.
- Some methodologies employ a **prototyping/agile** approach in an attempt to get a working solution produced sooner in the process that can be modified at later stages in the development.

Analysis

Key points:

- Before a problem can be solved it must be defined so that it is clear what must be produced.
- Once the boundaries of the problem have been established, a list of requirements will be drawn up in collaboration with the intended users of the system.

Key terms

Software development methodology A framework and set of principles that developers follow when developing a software product.

Prototyping Development of early sample products that allows the developers and users to experience what has been created with a view to informing future development.

Agile software development methodology A prototype methodology focused on developing incremental versions of a product quickly without large amounts of analysis and design beforehand.

- From this, a data model will be created to help visualise the scope of the software.
- Data-flow diagrams (DfDs) and entity-relationship diagrams are two examples of models that could be created at this stage.

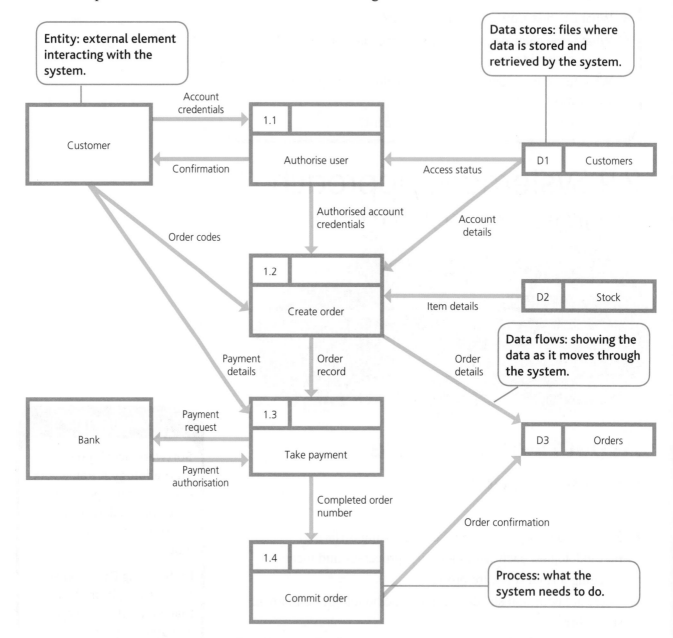

Figure 62 DfD of an ordering system found on a website

Design

Key points:

- Prior to constructing a solution, design of the components should take place to specify how the solution will work.
- Data structures to implement the data models will be considered.
- Algorithms will be planned for the expected processes.
- A plan of the modular structure for the solution will be decided.
- The human user interface will be designed.

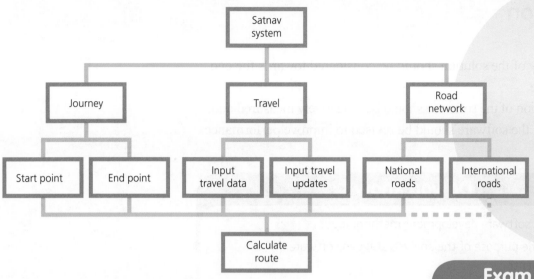

Figure 63 Identification of modules to be created in a satnav system

Implementation

Key points:

- The models and algorithms designed need to be implemented as data structures and code.
- This is presented in a format that the computer can understand.
- As a part of this stage, the developer will be testing that the implemented solution works as intended.
- As a part of this, user feedback may be considered to inform the development of the solution.
- As part of agile methodologies, the implementation of the product follows the **critical path**.

Testing

Completion of the implementation stage will require further testing to detect the presence of errors.

Table 24 **Types of testing**

Type	Description
Normal (typical) use	The solution is tested with normal data to check that the specified output is produced.
Boundary conditions	The limits of inputs are tested to ensure that all acceptable data can be used by the solution.
Erroneous data	Unacceptable input is used to check the solution rejects values it cannot process without affecting the operation of the solution.

As a part of a testing regime, acceptance testing should also be used to ensure the solution meets the requirements of the user.

Evaluation

Key points:
- The quality of the solution should be considered towards the end of the cycle.
- The operation of the software should be objectively measured and, if required, the software should be revised to improve performance.

Do you know?

1 What is a software development methodology?

2 What is the purpose of the analysis stage in software development?

3 What three types of testing should be performed on developed software?

4 Upon completion and testing of a solution, what should the user be required to do?

End of section 2 questions

1 Explain why the hexadecimal number system is useful in computer systems.

2 Describe why floating point numbers are limited to either a high range of imprecise values, or a smaller range of more precise numbers.

3 Outline the differences between system and application software.

4 Describe the advantages of using assembly language to write a computer program compared to developing software in a high-level language.

5 Identify the major components of a computer processor.

6 Explain the difference between immediate and direct modes of addressing.

7 Describe how a processor services an interrupt received by an item of hardware within a computer system.

8 Explain how Request to send/Clear to send (RTS/CTS) can be used to assist in the transmission of data across a wireless network.

9 Describe the differences between the computer threats worms, trojans and viruses.

10 Outline how subnet masks can be used to subdivide an IP v4 network.

11 Describe the Big Data terms volume, velocity and variety.

12 Identify the features of first-class objects.